AF422159

NONVIOLENT JOURNALISM

A humanist approach to communication

Pía Figueroa Edwards, Nelsy Lizarazo Castro,
Juana Pérez Montero, Tony Robinson, Javier Tolcachier

NONVIOLENT JOURNALISM

A humanist approach to journalism

© Pressenza, International Press Agency

Reproduction of any part of this book is allowed on the condition that credit to the source material is given in full.

ISBN: 979-8-218-18289-2

Front cover, graphic design and production:
Manthra Communications – Quito, Ecuador – info@manthra.ec
Milan Banach Nagy – Amsterdam, Netherlands –
milan.banachnagy@gmail.com

TABLE OF CONTENTS

PROLOGUE

Selected mainstream media trends over the last 50 years

And how the mainstream media became the largest single obstacle to an understanding of our complex world.

Jan Oberg[1]

Introduction

Academic writers should keep themselves in the background and let the analysis and interpretations speak for themselves. And it is not

---

[1] Jan Oberg PhD, is director of the Transnational Foundation for Peace and Future Research, TFF, in Lund, Sweden - https://transnational.live

that I need to speak about myself, but in this prologue – that I am honoured to have been asked to write – this is what I shall do in this introduction.

I've been a person used by the media in many countries over the last 50 years. I've written book reviews, feature and debate articles, columns and commentaries – first in printed dailies, radio and television, later also via the Internet.

I've written about my various experiences with the media in an online book titled, *Goodbye Peace. Worldmoires into a Peaceful Future* (Oberg, 2021)[2] – not memoires, but *worldmoires*, things that I have done and experienced around the world as part of my job as a professor, conflict analyst, mediator, writer, etc.

The chapter referred to contains a series of concrete cases of what I call MMMM – Mainstream Media Manipulation Methods, whereas what follows here is a summary of media trends: What has happened to the mainstream media over these almost 50 years?

My answers below are not the results of scientific investigation, they have a centre of gravity in Scandinavia where I live, and they are my subjective interpretations of these developments and experiences.

The main trends in the Western mainstream media

Quantity up, diversity down – there were much fewer media back then, but most of them practised the duty of diversity much better than even public service today; with local radio and TV stations mushrooming, the professional ambition of being as objective as possible and using diverse sources has practically vanished. Further, we have

---

[2] This essay is an edited and partly re-written version of the third chapter of my book, *Experiences with the media over 50 years*, which can be found online https://oberg.life/

witnessed an ever-increasing concentration of the dominant corporate mainstream media at the national and global level.

Quality decline and echo chamber culture – the professional quality has declined markedly. Today's media are produced with much less 'personality', love and professional pride. As a contributor, you are not cared for, and you no longer feel part of any media 'family.'

Three other aspects of this decline in quality deserve mention: One, studio hosts don't refrain from also becoming celebrities. Two, whereas earlier a journalist would interview an expert, they now often turn to another journalist. And three, editorial offices tend to end up in groupthink – repelling whatever does not fit the chosen narrative ('we cannot be wrong because so many others say the same'…).

Media pay for their own, not for expertise knowledge – today you are hardly ever paid for shorter articles or a television or radio comment. (As a matter of fact, I never had to take a loan for my education, I wrote for the media, commented on radio programs and gave public lectures). Freelance experts need to think of what assignments provide an income; those who have a monthly salary from a state institute or company don't have to do that.

When the media no longer pay, they are more likely to turn to experts with a permanent income who won't ask for a salary. This leads to a dominance of 'Establishment' perspectives and opinions rather than the freer, often more creative and genuinely independent perspectives. Overall, to know something about international affairs has become much less important in the media.

Less facts, more fake news and omission – the age-old rule of thumb that a piece of information must be confirmed by three sources independent of each other before it can be considered true and therefore publishable has succumbed to the fierce race of delivering the news first. I maintain and repeat as often as possible that *omission* is more damaging than *fake*. With some knowledge you may be able to sense a fake story; but thinking what news items were left out, what other perspectives and interpretations were not presented and what kinds of expertise was not used – all that is much more difficult.

Narratives have taken over – there is one, often meticulously constructed, version of the truth. Narratives are carefully constructed to make the superior West shine as the innocent player that is constantly challenged and therefore has to assume the modern version of the White Man's burden – the contemporary *mission civilisatrice* – of course accompanied by more or less fake arguments about promoting democracy and freedom, human rights, liberating women or deposing a "dictator."

Commercialisation – Commodification – news has become a commodity in the clicking and advertising media market economy; there is much more entertainment and mixed 'infotainment', and more sports prioritised more than before. Foreign policy pages have, in contrast, grown neither in quantity nor quality. In Scandinavia, for instance, a weekend edition may have 70 pages with only one page devoted to international affairs – and not beyond the EU or 8% of humanity.

Knowledge decline – media people with no education or experience in the field can cover international politics, security, war and peace. In the sections on sports, economy or, say, food – a certain minimum knowledge is required, if for no other reason than the readers, viewers and listeners themselves know something and can judge the quality of what they are being served. Tragically, it is as if any inexperienced journalist can be tasked with covering the most complex global affairs.

Homogenisation and uniformity – it used to be a major media professional drive to search for hidden stories, do investigative reporting and be the first to publish a new breaking story. Today, journalism has been reduced very much to editing the headlines and shortening the content of stories that originate from a few major Western news agencies and channels such as Reuters, Agence France Press (AFP), Associated Press, BBC, The Guardian and CNN and have already been watered down by the national news agencies before being published.

FOSI & MIMAC – FOSI stands for Fake news + Omission + Source Ignorance. *Fake news* is well-known and nothing new; invented stories have always been around servicing particular political purposes. What has grown exponentially is *omission*.

MIMAC stands for the Military-Industrial-Media-Academic Complex and is an extension of the Military-Industrial Complex (MIC), which President Eisenhower warned the US and the world about in his farewell address in 1961. This complex exercises an influence on today's society and policy-making in a much more significant and parasitic way than when he warned us. My main point is that today's (mainstream) media and relevant academia are well integrated into this complex – synergy and symbiosis. This explains why Western mainstream media are always on the side of Western weapons, warfare and militarism.

Unfree media and de-democratisation – every theory of Western democracy includes a rather free, independent press as the *sine qua non* of democracy. In that light, sadly, democracy is now a thing of the past. The symbiotic relations between the state/government and the media should be obvious to citizens by now.

Over the decades, I've witnessed how, step-by-step, there is less will to criticise and space for criticism of government policies. Further, it is true that we can all express ourselves in many more places than before – social media, comment fields, blogs, etc. – but power elites can ignore us in ways they did not dare to two-three decades ago. Now it seems they don't bother but leave that to their press spokespeople and public relations officers.

Paradoxically, all this is similar in tendency to 'the authoritarian state', which the West psycho-politically projects onto those non-Western states they consider dangerous.

The media 'culture' has moved away from public education – thus, between the 1970s, when I started doing media work, to around September 11, 2001, there existed a genuine, more frequent commitment to getting facts right; you were often asked to pedagogically explain to the audience what a conflict, for instance, was about. The media saw *public education* as an important task. Now *political correctness* has crept in everywhere. And there is *framing*: If I – the peace expert – give an interview to a newspaper, the editor will see to it that my views are 'explained' and, to some extent, countered by experts rolling out the necessary arguments from the ruling politically correct narrative.

Dialogue is out, debates dominate – *debates* are supposed to contain punchy arguments that end with 'I am right, and you are wrong! – that is, with *exclamation* marks. *Dialogues*, on the other hand, are explorative, more like conversations with the parties listening carefully and asking questions to better understand the other side – and therefore often ending with *question* marks.

Thus polarisation and confrontation, politics as a football match is the order of the day.

And wherever there is a conflict or war, there is a *media war* – the media act as megaphones for their own side, never searching for understanding of the underlying conflicts or explaining why the other side(s) do what they do.

It tends to be all about *positioning*: Which side are you on – defended with twitter-like statements in need of no substantive knowledge.

If you are seen as a dissident, *you get the critical questions* and have to defend yourself – never those operating inside that narrative or advocating war and armament.

In short, public service was thrown out of the window long ago. Most of it is a blatant *disservice* except, of course, to those in power and, thus, *elite service* for those inside the MIMAC.

Some possible causes and turning points

Admittedly, there is a risk that I have painted the past media world in a bit too rosy a light. Some of the above elements were present, or at least latent in the past – but they have become manifest and dominant now.

I believe that 9/11 was a turning point – and by that, I do not mean the attack itself but the US reaction to it, including the commencement of the Global War On Terror, GWOT, and the fundamental(ist), dichotomised worldview – "you are either with us or with the enemy."

So too the media.

This came a good decade after the end of the First Cold War around the 1990s, which the West triumphantly interpreted to mean that it had 'won' that war against Communism, the Soviet Union and its Warsaw Pact, and its system was, therefore, the best.

This combination of seeing oneself first as a *winner* and then *as a victim* – whether true or not – makes for dangerous policy-making in an era where the same West is declining on all indicators but the military and is bound to fall sooner rather than later as the leader of the outgoing unipolar Western-dominated world.

Given this 30-year perspective, it is not *that* strange that the West's mainstream media world has changed the way it has on various variables, as I have outlined above.

In summary, the end of the Cold War, September 11 and now the war in Ukraine – the most propagandist and politically correct media coverage I have seen (even worse than that of Syria) – are all turning points in the decay of our mainstream media. It is as if the decay of classical quality media work has been given full blast at every one of them.

Three constant characteristics – just more pronounced now

That said, I think there are at least three aspects that have remained the same over decades, but gotten more pronounced in the last 20-30 years:

Every war is always two wars – namely, the one on the battlefield and the one in the media.

The latter is about various kinds of mental-moral de(con)struction of truth and complexity, as well as of every feeling of "our" co-responsibility; it is about creating demons and promoting fear and hate – and making you forget everything about "unrealistic" options such as conflict analysis, mediation, negotiations, dialogue, peace plans, reconciliation, forgiveness, nonviolence and other – totally useless, of course! – methods with which to treat a conflict.

In terms of Ukraine today, the message is: "We" must win the war. But, nobody seems to be concerned about what that means for Ukrainians.

In the field of international politics, we must understand that the Western mainstream media do not *report* wars; they *participate* in them and *legitimize* them.

Those of us who often travel to places to see for ourselves have repeatedly made the same observation: The *media* image you travel out with about a conflict and war zone and its participants is extremely different from the *reality* image and understanding you travel back with after having lived in those zones.

I have never been to a conflict or war zone where I did not experience that. Strongly.

Western media has always been navel-gazing – in Scandinavia, for instance, you'll see extremely little news about the world outside your own country and the European Union, if it is not an earthquake or an accident in which your countrymen may have been involved, suffered or died.

G20 and G7 meetings, summits in BRICS and SCO – or the Belt And Road Initiative, BRI, which is the world's and history's largest cooperative project, high-level meetings in China's political system – you name it – are hardly mentioned or covered by professional, knowledgeable journalists. It's always been like that, structurally, but I believe that – in spite of globalisation – Western media have become even more provincial. It is as if there is an implicit belief that 'we do not have to learn from others because our role is to teach them.'

In this era of relative decline of The West, this structure and self-centred attitude lead only one way – to self-isolation and irrelevance in the eyes of The Rest.

War has always attracted the media more than peace – it's well-known that bad news is good news. Most people get depressed, feel powerless and otherwise overwhelmed when having watched their prime time news in the evening. I get the impression that more people today switch off – not least the younger ones – or limit their news checking to a certain time – hours before they are going to sleep.

Journalists always tell me that it is not their job to report on all the planes that land on time – but it *is* their job to report when a plane crashes. I accept that – but that is not the same as saying that news cannot also cover what would, generally, be deemed positive events and trends by millions of media consumers around the world.

Be this as it may, the media focus on war where they ought to focus on the underlying conflicts – but how do you get footage of them? It is easier to show destruction, dead bodies and soldiers fighting – just think of the World Press Photo competition.[3] It conveys that war is normal, part of human nature and probably impossible to eradicate.

We have war reporters, heroes reporting from the midst of death and destruction, putting their own lives on the line. But even before the war is over, they have left for a new war zone; they don't monitor peace and reconciliation or the emerging peaceful coexistence. We have virtually no mainstream coverage of, say, UN peace-keeping, how mediation and negotiations are carried out – or of reconciliation, forgiveness and peace processes.

------

[3] https://www.worldpressphoto.org/

The mainstream of the future!

Why have we ended up with these trends, this media crisis? My answer is that they have grown much worse concomitantly with the decline of The West vis-a-vis 'the Others'. The one losing power has less tolerance for diversity and criticism.

The distortions, narratives, propaganda and planted stories, outright lies and omissions have accelerated and become more desperate – more so for each (failed) intervention and war – and now even more money and energy is channelled into promoting the Western uniform, stereotype image of Russia and China.

However, I believe the systematic psycho-political projection of the West's own dark disinformation shadows unto 'the Others' will become increasingly difficult to sell. People will wake up to what I call their 'Pravda Moment' – the moment they see clearly the extent to which they have been taken for a political correctness ride.

That is likely to happen along with the breakdown of the system and decision-makers failing miserably in achieving any of all the goals they've set: re-arming tremendously *and* destroying Russia *and* paying the bills for it *and* devoting themselves to stop climate change *and* keeping China down *and* remaining the global leader of the outdated unipolar world *and* providing welfare, growth and good lives for their own citizens.

The West has set itself on mission impossible – while its decision-makers and mainstream media dine at the restaurant of the Titanic.

Perhaps peace, or nonviolent, journalism is an unfortunate term? It should not mean that the media shall, instead, promote peace. Rather, it means that quality journalism would cover the wars, violence and militarism as well as the underlying conflicts and, through an understanding of them, open up peace potentials.

The innovative works by Jake Lynch & Annabel McGoldrick (Peace Journalism, 2014), Jake Lynch & Johan Galtung (Reporting Conflict: new directions in peace journalism, 2010) and others like, e.g. Steven Youngblood (What is Peace Journalism?, 2017), convinced me years ago that a better type of journalism is possible. It's just not compatible with rampant militarism and macro-historical decline.

That much better way is the very message of this book and its marvellous, concrete and convincing examples. Since it is already being done, it must be possible. I think it's the mainstream of the future!

March 2023

INTRODUCTION

This book aims to reflect the first twelve years of collective effort of a non-profit organisation run by volunteers from the fields of journalism and communication: Pressenza, an international press agency with a nonviolent approach. It is on the basis of this approach and the process of developing the agency that we are able to present these pages to you. Twelve years of successes and failures, of experiments, alliances, and learning through dialogue with and the know-how of communicators, activists, and friends from academia who have provided us with the impetus to put down on paper the foundations and principles, the tools and suggestions that could shape a nonviolent approach to communication and journalism at the service of those who may find it useful. The team that worked on this production has been with the agency since its inception. We have lived and breathed this project, and that undoubtedly brings with it advantages and disadvantages to this text, which is why it is good for the reader to be aware of this fact.

As you will see, this production is halfway between a book and a manual. The reason is simple: we wanted to set out the elements that underpin the approach and also provide some tips that have helped us to put it into practice and to identify it in other allied media. Therefore, you will find examples taken not only from Pressenza but also from other media. We are not and do not aspire to be the "owners" of the content: we have learned from many people and in many environments. Our task is to integrate these learnings in the best possible way.

Who were we thinking of when we wrote these pages? Most especially in educational establishments where the new generations of communicators and journalists are being qualified. We would like this book to be useful in university lecture theatres, both for teachers and students. But we are also thinking of professionals in the field and activists in social collectives, movements and organisations whose agendas – also characterised by nonviolence – may find tools for dissemination in this approach.

This is the first edition. We reserve the right to improve it and, hopefully, in a little while, publish a second and third edition, etc. It is, therefore, a living publication.

Pía Figueroa Edwards, Nelsy Lizarazo Castro,
Juana Pérez Montero, Tony Robinson, Javier Tolcachier.

January 2021

Notes to the English edition

In January 2022, in a global meeting of Pressenza staff, a proposal emerged to take this book and develop an accompanying training course for students of journalism and social communication. The first step was to prepare an initial English translation of this book. Once this was completed, a team of six Pressenza editors, including two of the authors of this book, developed and delivered a training course of thirteen workshops.

This course took place in the summer of 2022. Eleven of those workshops were systematised and compiled into an accompanying book, *Nonviolent Journalism Training Workshops.*

With respect to the original Spanish text there are some intentional changes. Firstly, the Spanish text included a section of four ideas for workshops on some of the fundamental themes of Universalist Humanism that underpin our approach to journalism. With the development of the training workshops, this section became redundant.

Secondly, the Spanish edition logically included a high proportion of articles related to the Spanish speaking world at the end of each principle. This edition has attempted to include more articles connected to the English speaking world.

Finally, we commissioned a new prologue for this English language edition

For further information regarding any aspect of this book or for enquiries regarding our training course, please contact us at info@pressenza.com.

January 2023

THE HUMANISATION OF COMMUNICATION: THE CONCEPTUAL FOUNDATIONS OF NONVIOLENT JOURNALISM

The Human Being

There have been several attempts to explain what exactly it is that defines us as human beings.

Aristotle, for instance, described human beings as "political" or "social" animals, "*zoon politikon*". By identifying humans as a class of animals, he wanted to express the existence of a soul, or *anima*, as it was later expressed in Latin. Then by identifying humans as "social" an attempt was being made to relate to the fact that we are gregarious, that we seek each other out and build new relationships and social and cultural forms that are far removed from our initial starting point. Thus, what makes us human is differentiated from what is considered to be specifically natural.

Later on the Neoplatonic philosopher, Porphyry, defined man as a "mortal rational animal". By stating that we are rational, an attempt was being made to highlight a difference with the rest of the animated kingdom based on the use of logical faculties derived from the capacity for abstraction. The word "logic" comes from the Greek concept *logon*, which is very broad and difficult to pin down – corresponding to a certain capacity to discern, comprehend, think, differentiate, relate differences and reach conclusions. Of course *logon* also refers to the capacity to express all of this.

In more recent times, the Argentinian thinker Mario Rodríguez Cobos (1938-2010), better known as Silo, found efforts throughout history to define "the human being" to be lacking and attempted his own definition:

> *"To define human beings in terms of their sociability seems to be inadequate, because this does not distinguish them from many other species. Nor does capacity for work stand out as their most notable characteristic when compared to that of more powerful*

animals. Not even language defines them in their essence, for we know of numerous animals that use various codes and forms of communication. On the other hand, as each new human being encounters a world modified by others and being constituted by this intentional world, I discover their capacity for accumulation and incorporation into the temporal; I discover not simply a social dimension but a social-historical one. Viewing things in this way, we can attempt a definition of the human being as follows: Human beings are historical beings whose mode of social action transforms their own nature." (Silo, 1996)

The need to define what it is that makes us human may seem rather strange on the face of it until we understand that this definition, the conception we have of human beings, determines our behaviour and the way we relate to the world and to others. The attempt to develop a practice of nonviolent journalism is intrinsically linked to the journalist's conception of the human being.

Expansion of the temporal horizon

For animals, the environment is natural. For humans, the environment is also historical, cultural and social. The human environment is the adaptation of nature over millions of years in order to better resolve our immediate and longer-term needs. It is also something that can be transformed or conserved depending on the human capacity to develop intentions.

Human beings are not just concerned with the "present". They have a personal and social history, the result of things that happened in the "past". Human beings can also imagine the "future" and make plans for it. This human ability to defer into the future the responses to immediate stimuli received in the present, together with the ability to transmit our personal and social histories to other members of our species appear to be unique to *Homo sapiens*.

The Scheme of the Psychism and its Spatiality

In the human psychism, the *consciousness* is the apparatus which all human beings are endowed with and is what allows us to function in the world, acting as a mediator between the body and the environment. It is a mental space in which human beings are able to process stimuli and prepare and deliver responses into the environment.

In brief, human beings collect data from the world via the five external senses (sight, hearing, touch, taste, smell) and from inside the body via two internal senses: internal sensations of the body such as pain, temperature, muscular tension, blood pressure, etc. known as *coenesthesia*; and those resulting from bodily posture and movement, known as *kinesthesia*. Stimuli that are received by the senses are registered by the body as sensations and presented to the consciousness and structured into *perceptions*, while simultaneously recorded in *the memory*.

The consciousness, apart from recording new memories of received stimuli, is also constantly being presented with unsolicited data that is coming from the memory in the form of *memories*. The consciousness then structures the perceptions and memories into a *mental image* in such a way that a response can be given, or not given, depending on the *intentionality* of the individual (see below).

These responses can be expressed through the intellect, the emotions or through movement of the body and are generally a mixture of all three. All of these responses elicited by an individual are then recorded in the memory via the internal senses and the consciousness. This is the basis of learning which improves as the operations are repeated.

All of these operations are happening in a mental space where the consciousness operates, a space known as the *Space of Representation*. It is not possible to imagine anything without giving the mental images a spatial location in the space of representation. And we can observe that spatiality thanks to another mechanism: *reversibility*.

Reversibility

In the scheme of the psychism described above there are two important mechanisms when it comes to the idea of reversibility. One is connected to memory and how memories reach the consciousness. The other is connected to perception and how perceptions reach the consciousness.

In both cases there are two ways in which that data reaches the consciousness. One way is through a mechanical process in which the consciousness receives an unsolicited stream of memory and sense data. The other way is through an intentional process in which the consciousness goes looking for a particular memory, or using one particular sense, directing it in a search for something in particular.

In certain levels of consciousness the pathways for perception and memory become *reversible* and thus susceptible for transformation which depends on our intentionality.

Intentionality

Intentionality is a term from philosophy that pertains to the concept that mental states and images are about, directed towards or represent other things. Note that the meaning of the word intentionality should not be confused with the meaning of the word intention. (Jacob, 2019) The opening paragraph in the entry on Intentionality in *The Philosophy of Science: an Encyclopedia* gives us a useful starting point:

> *Some things are about, or are directed on, or represent, other things. For example, the sentence 'Cats are animals' is about cats (and about animals), this article is about intentionality, Emanuel Leutze's most famous painting is about Washington's crossing of the Delaware, lanterns hung in Boston's North Church were about the British, and a map of Boston is about Boston. In contrast, '#a$b', a blank slate, and the city of Boston are not about anything. Many mental states and events also have "aboutness": the belief that cats are animals is about cats, as is the fear of cats, the desire to have many cats, and seeing that the cats are on the mat. Arguably some mental states and events are not about anything: sensations, like pains and itches, are often held to be examples. Actions can also be about other things: hunting for the cat is about the cat, although tripping over the cat is not. This — rather vaguely characterized — phenomenon of "aboutness" is called intentionality. Something that is about (directed on, represents) something else is said to "have intentionality", or (in the case of mental states) is said to be an "intentional mental state".* (Byrne, 2006)

The word and concept in its usage more familiar to present day philosophy appear with Brentano at the end of the 19th century, yet the root of the term itself comes from ancient Greek, at least. Stoics such as Chrysippus used the term εντείνω, and this was taken up by Augustine and translated into Latin as *intentio*. (Caston, 1998).

Whereas Aristotle considers that vision and perception take place between a subject and an object directly (Aristotle, 1931), Augustine argues that there is something else at play, the perceiver's *intentio* which he characterises as a kind of striving or will, an intermediary between the object and cognitive faculty of the subject. In book XI of *On The Trinity*, Augustine identifies *intentio* with 'will' and 'love'. (Caston, 2019).

According to Brentano, consciousness is defined by the very fact of being intentional, directed towards something, referring to or showing something that is located outside itself, that is, it presupposes an object. In this way, intentionality gives consciousness significance, giving it meaning.

But it is Husserl, a disciple of Brentano, with whom the study of intentionality takes on a strict character, in his books *Ideas pertaining to a pure phenomenology and to a phenomenological philosophy* (Husserl, 1983) and *Cartesian Meditations* (Husserl, 1960). He considered that consciousness does not exist in a subjective vacuum, but is always "consciousness of something". Consciousness not only cannot be separated from the world of its objects, but it itself constitutes that world. It is the capacity we have to mentally direct ourselves towards objectives.

According to the Husserlian conception, it is not possible to understand how reality is constructed without a thorough understanding of the intentionality of the consciousness that constructs that reality. Husserl opened the way for thought to achieve independence from the materiality of phenomena.

The American psychologist Rollo May etymologically defines "intentionality" as movement in the direction of something, inclination, tendency. Central to this concept is "tend", which means to incline, to move towards. According to May, our acts are never purely the results of pushes from the past, they are the result of moving toward something. Furthermore, "to tend" also means "to take care of" – we tend our sheep and cattle, and we tend to ourselves. (May, 1974, p. 227)

May gives a simple example from everyday life:

> *"On the desk before which I sit lies a sheet of paper. If I have in mind to make some notes on the paper for my manuscript, I see the sheet in terms of its whiteness; has it already been scribbled upon? If my intention is to fold it into a toy plane for my grandson, I see the paper in its sturdiness. Or if my intent is to draw a picture on it, I see the rough, coarse-grained texture of the paper inviting my pencil and promising to make my lines more interesting. It is the same piece of paper in each case, and I am the same man responding to it. But I see three entirely different pieces of paper. It makes no sense, of course, to call this "distortion": it is simply an example of the infinite variety of meanings a given event, a given pattern of stimulus and response, can have. An intention is a turning of one's attention toward something. In this sense, perception is directed by intentionality."* (May, 1974, p. 233)

Similarly, we can say that memory, imagination, and human behaviour are driven by intentionality.

For his part, Silo, who founded the current of thought known as New or Universalist Humanism, considers that *"the consciousness is intentionality"* (Silo, 2003) and underlines the activity of consciousness, capable of transforming the world and itself according to its intentionality, stressing:

> *"...the primacy of the future over the present situation [...]. It is the image and representation of a future that is both better and possible [...] that allows the modification of the present and makes every revolution and all change possible. This is why the*

pressure of oppressive conditions is not in itself sufficient to set change in motion, rather it is necessary to realize that such change is possible and that it depends on human actions. This struggle is not between mechanical forces, it is not a natural reflex. It is, rather, a struggle between human intentions." (Silo, 1996)

Intentionality, spatiality and temporality of consciousness are key concepts to explain the structure of human life and to describe the phenomena of both the internal world and the environment around us. We often find that, in forecasting possible future scenarios for humanity, the question arises as to which scenario is more likely and which is less likely. As if the resolution of these alternatives were a statistical problem, independent of our attitude towards that future.

The humanist view emphasises the growing role of human intentionality in the process of planetary evolution and its decisive role every time there is a historical fork in the road. From this point of view, it is the intention to overcome pain and suffering, to overcome the spatial and temporal limits imposed by one's own body that gives impetus and direction to human history.

Violence

Intentionality expresses itself differently in each individual. Each of us has our own intentions, which sometimes makes it difficult to reach agreement. And in our differences we often seek to impose our own desires, our own vision of reality, forcing, clashing with or repressing the intentions of others, which frequently ends in violent imposition.

According to the World Health Organization (2002), violence is defined as:

"The intentional use of physical force or power, threatened or actual, against oneself, another person, or against a group or community, that either results in or has a high likelihood of resulting in injury, death, psychological harm, maldevelopment or deprivation".

However, prior to 2002, other authors also attempted definitions of violence. For Johan Galtung, a pioneer in the field of peace and conflict studies, *"Violence is present when human beings are being influenced so that their actual somatic and mental realizations are below their potential realizations."* (Galtung, 1969)

And he further explains:

"Violence is here defined as the cause of the difference between the potential and the actual, between what could have been and what is. Violence is that which increases the distance between the potential and the actual, and that which impedes the decrease of this distance. Thus, if a person died from tuberculosis in the eighteenth century it would be hard to conceive of this as violence since it might have been quite unavoidable, but if he dies from it today, despite all the medical resources in the world, then violence is present according to our definition."

Universalist Humanism takes this definition further.

"When people speak of violence, generally what they mean is physical violence, the most overt expression of corporal aggression. Other forms of violence, among others, economic, racial, religious, and sexual violence, can sometimes take place while their character is hidden, nevertheless resulting in the submerging or enslavement of human intention and liberty. In cases where these forms of violence are exercised openly, they are also

at times then applied through physical coercion. Every form of violence has discrimination as a correlate." (Silo, 2022)

Quoting further from the Dictionary of New Humanism:

Today, violence has penetrated all aspects of life: it appears continually and on a daily basis

- *In the economy (exploitation of some human beings by others, coercion by the State, material dependency, discrimination against women in the workplace, child labour, unjust taxes, etc.);*
- *In politics (domination by a single or small number of parties, the power of certain leaders, totalitarianism, the exclusion of citizens from real participation in decision-making, war, revolution, armed struggle for power, etc.);*
- *In ideology (the imposing of official viewpoints, the prohibition of free thought, subordination of the communications media to particular interests, the manipulation of public opinion, propaganda for ideas that are inherently violent and discriminatory but convenient to the ruling elite, etc.);*
- *In religion (subjection of the interests of the individual to clerical edicts, stringent thought-control, prohibitions against divergent beliefs, persecution of heretics, etc.);*
- *In the family (exploitation of women, dictatorial control or stifling of children, etc.);*
- *In education (authoritarianism of teachers, corporal punishment, prohibition of diversity in curricula and teaching methods, etc.);*
- *In the armed forces (arbitrariness of officers, unthinking obedience of soldiers, punishment, etc.);*

- *In culture (censorship, the prohibition of innovative currents and movements, prohibitions against publishing or performing certain works, edicts by the bureaucracy, etc.).*

Although women have come a long way towards emancipation, the discrimination, exploitation, contempt and exclusion that is exercised against them in the educational, political, spiritual and recreational spheres is still enormous, not to mention the murders, physical and sexual aggressions that millions of women suffer every day, naturalised and stripped of their intentionality by the macho perspective.

In the context of nonviolent journalism, violence is any attempt to supress the intentionality of other human beings. And what is important for nonviolent journalists is to recognise that physical violence generally is a symptom of the pain and suffering being caused by all the non-physical forms of violence. Quoting Silo again:

> *"So let's not be surprised when someone responds with physical violence if we've subjected them to inhuman psychological pressures or the pressures of exploitation, discrimination or intolerance. And if this response should surprise us it's either because we're an interested party of the injustice (in which case our "surprise" is also a lie) or because we only see the effects without noticing the causes that determine this explosion."* (Silo, 2014, pp. 152-3)

The subjugation of humanity is ultimately the source of violence, and we should note that this subjugation always begins with the denial of the other person's intentionality, be it subtle or crude.

Nonviolence

Nonviolence as a methodology for protesting against the violence of others can be found in the historical record going back over millennia (Swinden, 2006, pp. 228-241). Proponents include the founders of religions: Gautama Buddha, Jesus Christ and Zarathustra, and the most well-known practitioners of nonviolence in more recent times include Mahatma Gandhi (Fischer, 1951) and Martin Luther King (Carsen, 2001).

According to the renowned US political scientist, Gene Sharp, Nonviolent Action can be defined thus:

> *A technique of conducting protest, resistance, and intervention without physical violence by (a) acts of omission — that is, the participants refuse to perform acts which they usually perform, are expected by custom to perform, or are required by law or regulation to perform; (b) acts of commission — that is, the participants perform acts which they do not usually perform, are not expected by custom to perform, or are forbidden by law or regulation from performing; or (c) a combination of both.*

> *The broad phenomenon of nonviolent action has variously been referred to, in part or in full, by such terms as civil resistance, civilian resistance, nonviolent direct action, nonviolent resistance, passive resistance, positive action and satyagraha. Civilian struggle indicates the vigorous application of nonviolent methods.* (Sharp, 2012, p. xii)

Human consciousness is undoubtedly evolving over time. Despite the enormous levels of violence that people are subjected to everyday and the amount of time and money invested in it, humanity is not in the same conditions it was centuries ago. Advances are being made in eradicating violence, or at least in making certain forms of violence taboo and obsolete. We no longer throw our enemies into an arena to be eaten by lions, and slavery is illegal and is one of many elements enshrined into the Universal Declaration of Human Rights (United Nations, 1948). Furthermore, women have taken great strides towards equality, same-sex couples are able to marry in many countries and transgendered people are gaining increased acceptance and visibility.

In fact, it is possible to imagine that, as human consciousness evolves even further, the human capacity for empathy will develop to such an extent that violence will produce physical revulsion within human beings, with the corresponding somatic correlations. This would be an enormous advance for human societies. (Silo, 2014). A new consciousness capable of feeling repulsion towards any form of violence will lead human beings to assume nonviolent personal attitudes, even in the face of aggression. Of course, choosing a lifestyle dedicated to the pursuit of active nonviolence does not mean necessarily renouncing the right to defend oneself in the face of extreme physical violence, although Gandhi and Martin Luther King would not have encouraged it.

Violence is endemic in human societies. It pervades culture using the tools of religion, ideology, language, art, empirical science, formal science and cosmology. (Galtung, 1990) Thus, the work of the nonviolent activist, in whichever field they choose to work, is a permanent personal work on oneself, trying to identify those violent behaviours and attitudes that one has not intentionally chosen, but rather have been taught and transmitted to us over generations, and changing them.

For example, one such behaviour engrained into human beings is concerned with obedience to authority figures, even if those authority figures are exercising violence on others. In the 1960s, Stanley Milgram, the US social psychologist developed an experiment to see just how far people are willing to go when it comes to following those who are violent.

The experiment consisted of volunteers being called upon to participate in a study of memory and learning and being assigned the role of *Teacher*. Two other people who were informed organisers of the study then took the roles of *Experimenter* and *Learner*. The Teacher's role was to teach the Learner a list of word pairs. Every time the Learner made a mistake, the Teacher would administer an electric shock, every mistake meant the Teacher had to administer a shock of higher voltage.

The Teacher was always aware that the shocks would hurt and that the highest level shocks were dangerous. They were also aware that they could walk out at any time without any consequences, such as having to give back the money they received for participating. In reality, there was no shock. The Learner was in another room. The responses of the Learner to the Teacher's shocks were pre-recorded sounds to accompany every shock level. These included audible protests and banging of the wall indicating the extreme discomfort and pain of the Learner. Every time the Teacher had misgivings about the experiment and the damage being done to the Learner, the Experimenter stepped in with comments such as "please go on" and "the experiment requires that you continue."

Prior to the experiment, Milgram did some polling of psychology students to predict how many people would be prepared to administer the highest shock. The students predicted that between 1% and 3% of Teachers would be prepared to do so. In the experiment itself, 26 out of 40 (65%) were prepared to administer the worst shock of 450V and all of them administered shocks of 300V to the learners (for context, electricity in Europe has 220V). (Milgram, 1963)

Commenting on the experiment a few years later, Milgram said:

> *"The extreme willingness of adults to go to almost any lengths on the command of an authority constitutes the chief finding of the study and the fact most urgently demanding explanation. Ordinary people, simply doing their jobs, and without any particular hostility on their part, can become agents in a terrible destructive process. Moreover, even when the destructive effects of their work become patently clear, and they are asked to carry out actions incompatible with fundamental standards of morality, relatively few people have the resources needed to resist authority."* (Milgram, 1973)

This all begs the question, how often do we as human beings obey figures of authority who tell us to do something without question regardless of the consequences for others? Of course, the answer is: all the time, from the purchases we make, to the people we vote for, to tolerating the violent attitudes of others because we are too busy with other things. Civil disobedience is not easy.

Pietro Ameglio, the Mexican civil rights and peace activist, commenting on the work of Stanley Milgram, said:

> *"Civil disobedience is therefore not a destructive act, but on the contrary, it is a profoundly creative, innovative and active act; it is extremely original because it proposes a new social relationship that challenges the pre-existing order. It breaks an implicit relationship of collaboration, based on a legality, on a tacit agreement, which under these conditions, reproduces social injustice..."* (Ameglio, 1998)

Disobedience in the face of the diktats which generate social suffering, affecting human dignity and intentionality takes on the character of an essential human right. *"Nonviolence is therefore an ethic and a practice, a tactic of struggle"*, as the Argentinian humanist Lía Méndez points out in her book *Violence and Nonviolence*. (Mendez, 2015)

Today there are many daily examples of nonviolent action that are carried out in all part of the world, at different levels of social action, where individuals, institutions and organisations work on a daily basis with the aim of denouncing and eradicating different expressions of violence in society and promoting peace.

Nonviolent journalism

Nonviolent journalism gives space to concrete actions that raise awareness of the problem of violence, its true roots and its different forms of manifestation, while promoting exemplary actions aimed at eradicating these practices.

It is necessary to give visibility to these actions and to install the narrative of these actions through the media, which instead tends to make them invisible and only highlights the spectacle of violence. It is necessary to develop a journalism that prioritises exemplary nonviolent news, news that raises hope for a dignified world for all human beings.

All journalism, even if it claims to be objective, always comes with a point of view, a train of ideas which comes prior to the production of words or pictures. A nonviolent outlook is enabled by detecting in global, national and also local levels, those things that make a new path for humanity possible. It is an outlook that operates as a filter which allows us to decipher the facts that open the way to another reality.

As Aurora Marquina Espinosa points out in her book *Contributions for a Nonviolent Education:*

> *"It is necessary to enable the new generations to take a non-naïve view of reality. Perhaps we educators also need to empower ourselves and learn to observe, together with our students, how*

> *we construct our regard, from where we look, how this point of view can be changed and how so-called reality changes according to the internal and external conditions of the beholder".* (Marquina, 2003)

The aim of nonviolent journalism is to give visibility to the people and organizations who represent ways of living, actions and struggles which do not allow themselves to be swept along the unconducive path of the spiral of violence. It also highlights new forms of economics, based on solidarity and inclusivity.

It is a tireless search for news that has to do with conflict resolution, with overcoming all affronts to world peace and, at the same time, a permanent denunciation of everything that generates pain and suffering in the world.

Nonviolent journalism multiplies the echo of voices capable of establishing equality and parity, of inclusive actions, of the reversal of polluting processes and new forms of production based on clean energy. It advances towards the future creating narratives for the intentions and actions of human transformation towards a reality free from the many forms of oppression, from the many grotesque faces of violence.

The motor of history

Let us return finally to that possibility of choosing between different responses, the possibility of transforming situations, of transforming ourselves, of producing history.

What is the need that drives us to change things? What is the powerful engine that mobilises such an effort? There is a great deficiency that induces us to work to overcome it. This deficiency is called pain and suffering, depending on whether it is bodily or mental. That is why the human process is the story of the external and internal modifications that human beings produce in order to surmount pain and suffering.

In particular, to rebel against what seems to be a definitive conditioning – we are referring to finitude, to death: it is from this perspective that we understand how the full meaning or direction of human endeavour necessarily leads one to transform one's own inner nature, becoming the protagonist of a transcendent destiny.

We see then in this audacious, intentional being, whose consciousness is active and in open relationship with the world and other beings, capable of reflecting on themselves, their history and their future, we see a being that breaks the moulds and limits, leaving behind what is natural, what is conditioned, and moves towards the creative and indeterminate. We see the emergence of a transforming being who, in doing so, also transforms themselves. We see a horizon emerging that gives meaning to human life and which goes in search of freedom.

THE PRINCIPLES OF NONVIOLENT JOURNALISM

This section covers the general principles of nonviolent journalism, which constitute a basic, open and dynamic structure for approaching this style of communication. They are organised into three sections: those related to *information* itself; those related to the journalist's *point of view* or *look*; and those related to topics of *violence and nonviolence*. Following a brief introduction to each principle, we present examples of best practice to illustrate their application.

PRINCIPLES RELATED TO INFORMATION

Information is a public resource – communication is a human right

We constitute ourselves as human beings through our relationships with other people, through our interactions with others. Together we form a body, a social whole. For this social body to function and develop properly, it is necessary for information to circulate between the parts, for communication to flow in all directions.

In the 1970s, within the Non-Aligned Movement, the New World Information and Communication Order (NWICO) project emerged as an international attempt to reorganise global information flows in the search for independence, autonomy and cultural decolonisation.

Concerned about the consequences of the fact that most information always flows from the North to the South, NWICO and UNESCO promoted the creation of a commission to study the problem. In 1980 the report *Many Voices, One World* was published. (UNESCO, 1980)

This report analyses the relationship between the mass media (an expression of the times), power and democracy. It raises issues of interest that are still relevant today, including the role of the media as an instrument for the development of countries; the possibility of a flow of information that would work from all regions of the planet to compensate for the imbalance between the most and least developed countries; enhancing the variety of sources of information, the protection of journalists and the universal right of citizens and peoples to information.

Although this is when the defence of the universal right to information and communication began, the road has not been easy. Pressure from the big oligopolies, especially the US, meant that the NWICO project was soon abandoned and UNESCO replaced it with issues such as the democratisation of communication, the information society and digital inclusion.

Little by little, the concept of journalistic practice is broadening and the use of the term *communication* is expanding over that of *information*, as it responds more accurately to the practice of the profession, with the implications derived therefrom. The idea of the receiver as an essential active subject – without whom there is no exchange or production of collective meanings – acquires more and more weight, as do the rights that correspond to them. Therefore, a new reality is being shaped and recognised which is even more complex with the arrival of social networks.

In the last decade, the defence of freedom of expression and communication as a universal right has grown considerably. This has also strengthened the struggle against media concentration and the need for control of the media by grassroots organisations as a tool for empowerment, social transformation, change of mind-sets and of collective discourses and narratives.

What is at stake is who controls the collective narrative. Nonviolent journalism is a tool to visibilise and elevate grassroots voices.

Best practice

Headline:	Communication is a human right
Media:	Página 12
Author:	Leonardo D. Félix
Date:	November 5, 2019
Format:	Opinion piece
URL:	https://bit.ly/3u1TBs0

The author is the executive director of the Ecumenical Communication Agency and president of the World Association for Christian Communication for Latin America and he highlights several key points:

"Understanding communication as an inalienable human right for everyone is a basic fact that, although it seems obvious, needs to be revealed wherever the subjectivities of the great media monopolies are hegemonically imposed.

"Our existence results from the relationship with an other who lives their experience in the framework of different situations and values marked by economic situation, gender, ethnicity, geographical residence, educational credentials, etc. And if communicating implies sharing, the same process entails dialogue about the diversity of that shared experience and acknowledging the difference of that shared experience.

"Revealing this means that all the sectors that make up a society (including especially churches) cannot be above these basic principles and that they must necessarily dialogue, articulate and seek strategies that allow for democratic functioning. Otherwise, we would suspect with good reason that any struggle for respect for religious freedom, freedom of expression and freedom of information, is nothing more than an attempt to instrumentalise

the denial of rights and impose thoughts as if they were unique in their interpretation and content."

The article notes the factual and unacceptable appropriation of communication as a result of media editorial lines, at the same time as it precisely indicates the need to recognise and talk about differences. In this sense, a clear openness to diversity is evident, and a warning is given about the disastrous dogmatism that uses freedom of expression as a subterfuge to impose a single way of thinking. The inherent nonviolent direction of informational multiplicity is thus made explicit.

Headline:	Statement by ALER on the right to communication in Ecuador
Media:	Pressenza
Author:	Pressenza Ecuador
Date:	February 20, 2017
Format:	Press release
URL:	https://bit.ly/3lvM1v0

In this article, the Latin American Association of Radio Education (ALER), through its president Leonel Herrera Lemus, draws attention to the possible modification of the Ecuadorian Organic Law of Communication in favour of private interests. He points out:

"Trying to repeal this law, which is protected by the Constitution of Ecuador, which recognises the human right to communication and is seen in Latin America and the Caribbean as a positive reference in the struggle for the democratisation of communication and the right of peoples to communicate, would constitute a worrying step backwards in the democratic life of the country.

"Tendering for radio frequencies... is a mechanism that is supported by article 108 of the Organic Law on Communication and allows, for the first time in the history of the country, for citizens,

peoples and communities, through their organisations, to legally have their own community media..."

In addition to denouncing media concentration, the press release defends the community's right to communication:

"There is an attempt to violate this right by those who advocate for the repeal of the law and seek to reform it in order to maintain the current media status quo. It is pertinent to point out that freedom of expression is not only the right of those who currently own one or more media outlets, but is a right of society as a whole. Therefore, the tender process must continue and be respected.

"In recognition of the long process promoted by social organisations and movements to have the law consider the fundamental aspects of the right to communication, ALER echoes the Report of the Inter-American Commission on Human Rights (IACHR) Rapporteur for Freedom of Expression on the recommendations to limit media concentration with the objective of guaranteeing freedom of expression. The document states that: 'Pluralism and diversity of media outlets is of particular importance for the full and universal exercise of the right to freedom of expression. In terms of a recent Inter-American Court ruling, the protection of pluralism is not only a legitimate aim, but also an imperative'."

Headline:	Intellectual Property Monopolies Block Vaccine Access
Media:	Inter Press Service
Author:	Anis Chowdhury and Jomo Kwame Sundaram
Date:	December 15, 2020
Format:	Opinion piece
URL:	https://rb.gy/3y4xdf

When considering the first part of this principle, information is a public resource, we hold it to be self-evident that there is no information in the world that has not been dependent on the action of human beings since pre-historic times. The principles of conservation, transportation and production of fire were developed not by elite scientists, but by tribes working in the interest of everyone. Without the collective efforts of every human being throughout history, scientists, doctors, inventors, entrepreneurs, engineers, philosophers, and so many others would be unable to make the advances possible today. When Isaac Newton said "If I have seen further, it is by standing on the shoulders of giants," he perfectly summed up this principle. In this context, not allowing information to be freely available contributes to the growing dehumanisation of the world's population.

One of the areas in which the results of not applying this principle is alarming is the area of medical patents. The COVID-19 pandemic dramatically highlighted the violence inherent in restricting access to information that should be a public resource.

In this article, which first appeared in Inter Press Service, the authors first provide context.

> *"Just before the World Health Assembly (WHA), an 18 May* open letter *by world leaders and experts urged governments to ensure that all COVID-19 vaccines, treatments and tests are patent-free, fairly distributed and available to all, free of charge."*

Some world leaders clearly understood the problem of subjugating information to the cause of profit:

> *"Leaders of Italy, France, Germany, Norway and the European Commission called for the vaccine to be 'produced by the world, for the whole world' as a 'global public good of the 21st century', while China's President Xi promised a vaccine developed by China would be a 'global public good'."*

Health activists understand the impacts of this not being the case:

"Many more people will be infected and may die without vaccinations, warns the People's Vaccine Alliance, advocating equitable and low-cost access."

Yet the world's pharmaceutical companies would prefer enormous numbers of people to die rather than allowing others to access their knowledge to save lives. And this despite the fact that funding for their vaccines came from public money.

"Pfizer has received a US$455 million German government grant and nearly US$6 billion in US and EU purchase commitments. AstraZeneca received more than £84 million (US$111 million) from the UK government, and more than US$2 billion from the US and EU for research and via purchase orders."

Nonviolent journalism's role is to highlight this violence and to denounce those who exercise it and are complicit with it, after all...

"Indeed, as Proudhon warned almost two centuries ago, 'property is theft'."

Permanent development of knowledge

The search for knowledge is an essential activity of the consciousness that characterises humanity and acts as a support for the transformation of the world and of each individual. From a historical perspective, knowledge is used for avoiding and overcoming pain and suffering. Therefore, one of the main interests of nonviolent journalism is to contribute to the dissemination and transmission of knowledge.

The concept of knowledge is much broader than that of science, which is one of its manifestations. Even when we popularise science, we seek to provide a universal look, showing the contributions of different marginalised cultures. This is in order to break through the walls erected by the violent appropriation, monopolisation and with-holding of other knowledge by Western culture.

Knowledge is the fruit of the collective effort of humankind through-out its history. It is the common property of all human beings, both in terms of the rights and the benefits derived therefrom.

Nonviolent journalism does not support the vested interests of companies, states or institutions of any kind in the transmission of knowledge from any of their fields. On the contrary, nonviolent journalism transmits knowledge as accurately as possible and denounces any attempt to hegemonise, limit or impede the growing and collective process of acquiring knowledge.

The evolution of knowledge is a central issue for nonviolent journalism which, based on the humanist attitude, recognises and encourages its development beyond what is accepted or imposed as absolute truth.

In this way, maximum interest is placed on the debate on novel alternatives, theories and projects. No attempt is made to hide a conservative or regressive spirit behind the curtain of formality or supposed rigour.

The acceleration and multiplication of knowledge requires a constant updating of the knowledge of communicators in order to incorporate content that allows for an updated and comprehensive understanding of any phenomenon.

Knowledge is a social asset. That is why nonviolent journalism is committed to its socialisation and to working tirelessly for equal access to it.

Best practice

Headline:	Journey into the unknown: The new generation of telescopes promises...
Media:	Cubadebate
Author:	Reinaldo Taladrid
Date:	March 27, 2019
Format:	Interview
URL:	https://bit.ly/3ul5NVd

"Reinaldo Taladrid: Welcome to 'Journey into the Unknown.' We are seeing as a species what humans never dreamed of seeing and we are on the verge of beginning to see unimaginable things. Through what? Telescopes. That's what we'll be talking about today.

"Dr Oscar Álvarez Pomares: Of course it is. The new generation of telescopes that is coming now is going to explore unprecedented things. For example, they will be able to detect extrasolar planets, study their atmospheres and see if there is any life or any trace of life on those planets, not planets in the solar system, but planets around other stars. Those are the new telescopes, the ones that are coming now, which are not there yet.

"Reinaldo Taladrid: Future... what do you think we will be able to see or know with these new telescopes, especially the JAMES WEBB and that kind of telescope?

"Dr Oscar Álvarez Pomares: The whole space race is somehow aimed at detecting conditions of life around other stars.

"Reinaldo Taladrid: Definitely, human beings have to go and live somewhere else.

"Doctor Oscar Álvarez Pomares: Human beings are definitely going to do this as they have done throughout the ages. This is not

new, in other words, this is the history of humankind since it began and came out of the caves, it is always expanding and broadening its horizons. There will come a time when we will reach the Moon, Mars, there will even be a time when we will have to leave the solar system, perhaps to another satellite of the solar system, to a nearby star, and there will be a time when we will move from our galaxy to another galaxy. I see that as inevitable. If you study the history of mankind, you will see that this has happened on other scales."

The headline of this interview already shows an openness to what is new, to what is yet to be known. At the same time, it expresses the intention of disseminating relevant knowledge to large audiences. The piece points out the dynamics of knowledge and expands its possibilities on the basis of its inherent condition as a public asset.

Headline:	A necessary debate for Latin America. The social economy of knowledge or the commercialisation of knowledge?
Media:	ALAI
Author:	Juan José Romero Salazar
Date:	September 9, 2020
Format:	Opinion piece
URL:	https://bit.ly/3D6qyrv

"The Social Economy of Knowledge questions the privatising approach that has been given to intellectual property with digital business models and new digital products. From this perspective, the Social Economy of Knowledge becomes an area of study that aims to produce tools to make inclusion in the knowledge society viable, and to promote the emancipation of humanity with freedom of access to information, which should not be restricted or suppressed by economic interests of the minorities that control the large media corporations. In the field of research, it is a mat-

ter of turning knowledge into an infinite, public and open re-
source, whose dissemination serves to build a citizenship of soli-
darity."

This extract addresses the currently dominant ownership models of new digital technologies, and, based on this analysis, proposes alternatives of knowledge at the service of humanity as a whole, without restrictions arising from economic interests.

Headline:	Interview with Bárbara Rojas: "We are trying to look for another planet with the characteristics of Earth"
Media:	Pressenza
Author:	Pressenza, Chile
Date:	November 15, 2020
Format:	Interview
URL:	https://bit.ly/3LcT51s

"We, as scientists, have a responsibility to report what we are doing. At the moment, with the techniques we have, it is much easier to find – for example – a second Earth around a red dwarf than around the Sun.

"Pressenza: So you are looking for another planet Earth?

"Exactly, that's what we're trying to do and characterise that system. At the moment we haven't found any planets that are like the Earth, in the sense that they orbit a star like the Sun, that take a year to orbit it, and that have the same physical properties as the Earth, we haven't found them yet. What we have found are objects that are similar to the Earth in mass and size, and most of those are found in red dwarfs. That's what I like to study."

This article is informative and provides an update on the state of astronomical research in a language understandable to non-specialist audiences. This dialogue is part of the documentary, *They sense it will be dawn*, (Feres, 2019) which brings together, over the course of several interviews, the work of Latin American women at the forefront of different fields of science and technology with the aim of contributing to a common social and environmental future. By showing women in avant-garde roles of advanced social construction, it promotes the positioning of a new look, far from outdated stereotypes of the patriarchal order.

The grassroots as a source of information

The sources that journalism uses to transform content into news reports, feature stories, interviews, or any other format are perhaps the key to the reliability and trust that the produced information generates in your audience.

That sources should be serious, rigorous and that their processing should seek to contrast and confirm data are some of the basic lessons learned in journalism training. Even so, paradoxically, we live in an era plagued by fake news, rumours that are transmitted as information, unsubstantiated claims, and an enormous amount of content that circulates rapidly through social networks and that, frequently, is of unknown provenance.

At the same time, largely due to the accelerated advance of information and communication technologies, a large number of people are circulating 'first-hand' content, in other words, from places where events are happening, with testimonies from those who are experiencing them and with images that give an account of what is happening. Thus, multiple voices, faces and facts of daily life are made known from the most diverse corners of the planet. These are issues that lead to debates about the role of journalism.

That sources of information should be the voices of the people, organised or not, is a principle that in Latin America and the Caribbean was established particularly in the second half of the last century, based on the postulates of popular communication, a direct heir to the ideas of popular education and the thought of Paulo Freire: popular, in the sense of aimed at ordinary people, as opposed to specialists. (Freire, 2005) (Brito Lorenzo, 2008)

Since then, the idea of communication and journalism as horizontal and participatory activities, aimed at allowing the voices silenced by power in multiple spheres of reality to be expressed and heard, has given identity to a strong and enduring movement not only from the grassroots but also from multiple alternative expressions.

This movement arose as a response to the mainstream media's practice of always interviewing and giving prominence to the same people, silencing the voices of poor rural communities, local neighbourhoods and social organisations.

Placing the grassroots as the primary source of information is one of the central principles of the approach proposed in this book and is based on reaffirming the importance of the active consciousness and intentionality of every human being in dealing with the facts and the reality in which they live.

The reality we seek to show comes from the multiplicity of people's experiences in diverse societies, from the many points of view of those who constitute those societies: the unceasing diversity of the grassroots.

This is certainly not the only possible point of view, but it is the first, the starting point, the one that is directly linked to life, giving rise to multiple alternative looks and truths.

Priority is given to news that derives from ordinary people, from collectives and movements, from simple voices working together, and from the community on a daily basis, denouncing the daily violence imposed on them, for the transformation of their living conditions and those of others.

Giving people back their voices endows communication and journalism with a renewed dignity and identity, or as Jesús Martín-Barbero puts it:

> *"...only then would we begin to understand that neither semiology nor information theory can tell us what communication is in Latin America, but only by listening to how people experience communication, how people communicate. If we accept this, we are accepting that we have to arrive at the theory but from the processes, from the opacity, from the ambiguity of the processes. This makes us much more humble, much more modest, and much closer to the real complexity of life and communication."* (Martin-Barbero, 2012)

Visibilising collective voices and efforts, those from below, is rare in the mainstream media, which tends to portray poverty and pain in a way that victimises and degrades people.

Likewise, activities carried out in solidarity with others and struggles for better living conditions are treated superficially, turning them into light-hearted stories, frivolous articles that empties them of their true meaning.

It is crucial to elevate these voices and these struggles, to characterise them as a source of dignified and reliable, legitimate and truthful information. These are the grassroots protagonists who are the seeds of the society we aspire to.

Best practice

Headline:	We need to teach people how to fight against violence and racism
Media:	La Poderosa
Author:	Silvino Báez
Date:	December 2, 2020
Format:	Testimonial
URL:	https://bit.ly/3JEliNd

The author of the article is directly involved in the situation: he is the father of Fernando Báez Sosa, a young Argentinean boy murdered by a group of rugby players in January 2020. The media outlet gave him space to narrate the facts and the experience in his own voice:

> *"This week we have seen the racist and xenophobic comments of several rugby players, and everything they said should be taken into account by the justice system. On 18 January in Villa Gesell, a group of rugby players took Fernando away from us and we are still waiting for the judge to set a trial date for the eight murderers who are now in prison. They beat my son because of racism and they were prepared to kill someone; if it wasn't him, it would surely be someone else. It was out of hatred; maybe they think that way and they felt superior because they were blond, and Fernando had brown skin. If they had thought about the other person, none of this would have happened."*

Silvino's voice paints a picture of racism and xenophobia, which is at the root of his son's murder, and he denounces the slowness of justice.

He writes from his pain but also from a place founded on nonviolence:

> *"It's been almost 11 months since they killed him and since then our life has taken a big turn; we're not like we used to be, we*

miss those happy moments with him all the time. Today we are like we were the first day he was gone: my wife and I work to try to distract ourselves and occupy our minds, but we can't even listen to music, because there are songs that remind us of Fernando and our hearts can't take it. We feel that it is still hard to accept that we don't have him anymore. There is a huge void and our day to day life is living without a future, without plans, we have lost our way. I dreamed of seeing him grow up, of seeing him finish college, but no more... I can't dream anymore. Others crossed his path and mercilessly killed him brutally with punches and kicks.

"I have nothing against rugby or any other sport; I just think it's necessary to teach people to fight against violence and racism, because those who kicked him to death have no shame in hitting a kid who is unconscious on the ground. And all those kids who wouldn't let his friends help him, all those who prevented them from passing are equally shameless. Today we need justice and we need education in sport, so that there will be no more cases like Fernando's."

The author bears witness to his and his wife's pain, while stating his position and proposing alternatives: an article from the voice of a protagonist with a nonviolent approach.

Headline:	Testimonies of four indigenous women leaders from Peru
Media:	Servindi – Intercultural communication for a more humane and diverse world
Author:	Servindi
Date:	March 14, 2020
Format:	Testimonial
URL:	https://bit.ly/3Lejmwu

The article is constructed from the voices of four women. The Peruvian Amazon and its problems reach the readers through their words and bring us closer to their reality.

Delfina denounces different forms of violence against women, the ineffectiveness of the Western justice system, as well as the challenge that this type of violence constitutes for indigenous justice:

"Delfina Catip, member of the National Board of Directors of the Interethnic Association for the Development of the Peruvian Jungle (AIDESEP), denounces the fact that Peruvian government institutions do not understand the situation of violence against indigenous women. Despite coordination with the Ministry of Culture and the Ministry of Women's Affairs, it has not been possible to define effective mechanisms for dealing with the various forms of violence against indigenous women, says Delfina Catip, a native of the Awajún people. Ignorance of their customs, bureaucratic obstacles tainted with corruption, and ignorance of how to guide them to file a complaint of violence in their mother tongue, hinder justice for indigenous women. Catip reveals that in the deep jungle of the Peruvian Amazon, violence against indigenous women is hidden and lost in oblivion. The Amazonian leader maintains that indigenous justice is still a challenge to become a legal reality. Indigenous justice must be strengthened with effective coordination from the various ministries to enable it to be clearly regulated, in accordance with their customs."

Melania, on the other hand, highlights the domestic issue and the participation of indigenous women in political decision-making spaces:

"Melania Canales of the Quechua people, a native of Ayacucho, and president of the National Organisation of Andean and Ama-

*zonian Indigenous Women of Peru (ONAMIAP), affirms that in-
digenous women in Peru carry a history of violence on their skin.
For the Quechua leader, the ancestral patriarchy has been
strengthened by the colonial era, in which indigenous women
have not been free to make decisions. Canales questions the fact
that women are exploited with domestic tasks that are not recognised. To equalise the rights of indigenous women in Peru,
Melania Canales sees the urgent need to ensure the real representation of 50% of women in the State, as was proposed with
the gender quota law for regional and local governments. The
ONAMIAP representative denounces that women are only used
to appear on electoral lists because there is no law of alternation
that guarantees that indigenous women can occupy decision-
making positions. Once representation with gender equity and
alternation in the seats of the Legislative Power is achieved, they
would immediately seek the return of the three "I's" in the Political Constitution to strengthen the territorial security of the communities".*

Serafina affirms the above issues and calls for action in the struggle
for women's rights:

*"Serafina Huamán is president of the Network of Indigenous
Communicators of Peru, Cusco branch, and maintains that economic dependence on their spouses is a factor that blocks their
autonomous initiatives and leads them to suffer violence at the
hands of various agents. The indigenous communicator affirms
that women in rural areas need to raise this issue with the different levels of government in order to reduce violence and allow
them to contribute to the economy of their homes. In terms of
gender equality, Serafina Huamán highlights the progress
achieved for women, both in leadership positions and in public
and power positions. The Quechua communicator attests that*

the achievements for women have meant enduring various humiliations, even in their own homes, in order to be recognised, as she experienced first-hand. Huamán says with conviction that, in order not to back down in the struggle for their rights, women must lose their fear and show that they are capable."

Finally, Elva describes situations of violence against women and opens up alternatives for justice that include the use of indigenous languages:

"From the deep jungle of Peru, Elva Yaun, leader of the Regional Organisation of Indigenous Peoples of the Northern Peruvian Amazon (ORPIANP), testifies that violence against indigenous women has a child's face and often takes place in the home. It is a sad and stark reality, but she says that sometimes it is the parents themselves who rape their daughters.

"Girls in the Amazon are sentenced to live in fear of being used as sexual objects. Violence in the Amazon affects women of different generations who are assaulted in their individual and collective human rights. For Awajun and Wampis women it is very difficult to find justice due to the absence of the Peruvian state, so they have to take justice into their own hands. This results in episodes that can lead to the loss of their lives.

"To stop this violent and unjust scenario, Elva Yaun calls for co-ordinated regulation between the communities and the prosecutor's office to punish acts of violence and enforce respect for the rights of girls and women.

"She points out that, although there are currently police stations and the Public Prosecutor's Office, they do not fully perform their functions because they are unaware of the reality of the situation.

*On the contrary, the authorities are corrupted and end up sup-
porting the perpetrators instead of supporting the victims. Elva
Yaun sees the need for a translator and interpreters in the public
offices where justice is dispensed, so that the authorities understand the victims and can find justice in their complaints."*

Often, the direct testimony of protagonists of an event does not require additional commentary. The journalist's task, then, is essentially to establish a certain order or sequence in order to facilitate
reading.

Headline:	Dedicated Lives 6. "I am not Pascale, I am Women in Front"
Media:	Pressenza
Authors:	Angel Burbano and Runa Sanabria
Date:	June 30, 2016
Format:	Interview
URL:	https://bit.ly/3NgUGVd

This interview brings to the table the perspective of the group
Women in Front, through the words of one of its members, Pascale
Laso. The headline itself speaks of a collective voice, from the grass-
roots.

The interview highlights a new perspective of feminist organisation,
the value of collaboration, political identity, new forms of dialogue,
community life towards a shared horizon: happiness. All this from the
voice of one of its activists:

*"Pressenza: Why does Pascale help other women pursue happi-
ness through education?*

*"Pascale: Help is not the word. I am a militant, I work as an ac-
tivist. I am not helping because that concept comes from the
powers that be. I build spaces for other women and it is as enriching for me as it is for them. Even if I were a shoemaker, I*

would have done it from my trade, for me the importance lies in building collective spaces."

The interviewee emphasises the grassroots character of the collective and proposes new forms of social relations from there:

"Pressenza: Was this the reason why Pascale decided to work with different women: in prisons, of different age or ethnicity?

"Pascale: I am not Pascale, I am Women in Front. Women in Front is a POLITICAL COLLECTIVE, we are not individuals. So when we decided to enter the prison and show solidarity, we did it as a political collective with the women who are there. When we decided to set up the school, we did it as Women in Front. We have a group that is working more on the prison issue.

"Pressenza: What is the importance of dialogue for Women in Front?

"Pascale: It is a loving dialogue. I believe that dialogue builds things and the possibility of real dialogue builds other possibilities of knowledge. When a woman comes to school, I feel that she has a lot of knowledge and that she tells me all that knowledge. Nobody understands the city better, for example, than a woman who sells on the street. I am not talking from a superior position, what they bring to school is as important as what I bring to school.

"What we are doing here is Women in Front. This school is going to be five years old and with the contribution of all the women who come here, because they are not the same. At the beginning there were 4 of us, then 6, and now there are 11 more women from the collective. Every woman who comes contributes in a different way, but there is a desire to be able to speak in a diverse

way, to generate links, to create a happier present for all of us. We currently have 30 women."

Beyond information: action

Various schools of thought in journalism insist that its task is to inform. Much has been written about content, the conditions for it to be reliable and truthful, the care taken over sources, etc. This forms a certain basis of agreement between even the most conventional journalism and the multiple alternatives that have been deployed and proliferated over time.

Over the last 20 years, these alternative forms of journalism have exploded with much greater diversity and strength, largely as a consequence of the development of information and communication technologies, but undoubtedly also because of the emergence of previously invisible social actors and due to the struggles for the right to communication for all.

The principle discussed in this section proposes that, in addition to reporting, it is up to us to act. Journalistic work is in itself an action, and yet the principle begins with: Beyond information... What is this *beyond* to which we refer? What is the *action* that is beyond information in the proposed approach?

We are talking about action that engages us with communities, social movements, collectives, organisations and even institutions that consistently and permanently seek to transform their living spaces, from the closest to the furthest away, in a nonviolent direction. It is not only about covering the stories of the social actors of the future, but also about walking with them. For us, accompanying a march, a strike, a nonviolent action is not only a matter of profession, but of solidarity and active participation.

This principle, like the vast majority of those we propose, is shared by those who do journalism at the grassroots level and the people's agenda. Moreover, it also marks the identity of many more recent journalistic proposals, many of them developed by young collectives that have made communication an exercise in militancy, reclaiming its transformative purpose: mobilising stories, discourses, narratives and meanings that are often in dispute.

> *"What we are doing is fighting together: we are committed to collectivisation, to collaboration between media. We believe that this is what will change reality. To work together is to hold assemblies, meetings, grassroots groups to articulate ourselves. This is the only way we can change history. Midia Ninja alone is not going to change Brazil; we have to work together with society."* (Vázquez, 2018)

Once again, we confirm the impossibility of journalistic objectivity, this time positioning ourselves in a place of commitment to proposals and practices that seek, in a nonviolent way, to denounce and overcome any form of violence.

Best practice

Headline:	Solidarity with Julian Assange
Media:	Pressenza
Authors:	Pressenza Berlin
Date:	September 12, 2019
Format:	Press release
URL:	https://bit.ly/3LiAQl3

This article is a call to action in support of Julian Assange. The author takes a position and moves into action, joining forces with other media and organisations. This shows that taking a position and taking action implies alliances and joining forces with others.

The article first provides some context:

"Journalist Julian Assange has been held in solitary confinement in an English high security prison for weeks. He is in solitary confinement, which is a form of torture in accordance with all human rights.

"Berlin friends and Julian Assange's supporters have long met every Wednesday in front of the U.S. Embassy at the Brandenburg Gate for a vigil. On this occasion there is money to be collected for the victim of the US's megalomania. Because Julian needs money: for the lawyers and the organization around a life in detention. Donations are also a material sign of solidarity.

"Come to the U.S. Embassy in Berlin on December 11, 2019 at 19:00 hours. Let's bare our teeth to the silent cartel. Help collect donations for Julian.

"Donations for Julian Assange are possible online through the donations page https://defend.wikileaks.org/donate"

Headline:	The Beginning of the End of Nuclear Weapons premiered in New York
Media:	Pressenza
Authors:	Tony Robinson
Date:	June 14, 2019
Format:	Photo story
URL:	https://rb.gy/4bvbis

Just by publishing such material, this already marks a divergence from mainstream journalism.

Since its very inception, Pressenza International Press Agency has closely followed the topic of nuclear disarmament and has found itself to be almost alone among the world's media organizations to do so. Yet this topic is so vitally important for the very survival of life on the planet and the continued development of human consciousness.

The task of nonviolent journalism is to inform people about the topic, providing useful arguments and data with which they can dispute the dominant narratives in the media surrounding nuclear weapons which are all about "national security" and "deterrence" and completely dismissive of the humanitarian consequences of any use of nuclear weapons and the devastating effects on human beings and the environment. To this end, having accumulated a wealth of knowledge and friendships with activists in the anti-nuclear movement, the logical step in 2018, after the International Campaign to Abolish Nuclear Weapons was awarded the Nobel Peace Prize, was to make a documentary film. The film premiered in New York in June 2019.

> *"An audience of around 70 people, made up of activists, journalists and two people from the Permanent Mission of Mexico to the UN gave a very enthusiastic response to the film which tells the story of the history of the bomb, anti-nuclear activism and the Treaty on the Prohibition of Nuclear Weapons in the words of people who have dedicated their lives to making them illegal. It ends with examples of how anyone can get involved in order to make a difference and build up the stigmatisation of nuclear weapons so that governments sign and ratify the treaty as soon as possible."*

Producing and publishing material such as this is a perfect example of how journalism can move beyond its traditional role of informing audiences and inspire people to activism and provide a pathway for getting involved.

Headline:	Europe accepts the legislative initiative of citizens demanding a Universal Basic Income for all its residents
Media:	Pressenza IPA
Authors:	Ángel Bravo
Date:	May 29, 2020
Format:	News report
URL:	https://rb.gy/qiqbtz

Another topic that receives virtually no space in conventional media outlets is the topic of Universal and Unconditional Basic Income, a proposal by which every human being, just by existing, would be able to access a basic level of income to guarantee such rights as housing, healthcare, education, security in old age and a dignified standard of living.

Again, simply by giving space to such material, nonviolent journalism marks its radical divergence from mainstream journalism. This article, written by the coordinator of the European Citizens Initiative in Spain, Ángel Bravo not only informs readers about two topics that may be new to many: A European Citizens Initiative and Universal Basic Income, it also provides a way for readers to get involved.

> *"An ECI is a kind of popular legislative initiative which is presented to the European Parliament for discussion and possible approval. It involves collecting a million signatures and identity documents from European citizens who support the initiative, in at least 7 countries of the European Union (EU)."*

By giving a voice to one of the protagonists of the initiative, this article also diverges from other media outlets who generally criticise the proposal for being naïve and utopian. As if Utopia were a bad idea and something to avoid striving for at all costs!

> *"Until then, work will focus on forming a signature collection platform. And that is why people and groups of all kinds are*

encouraged to participate, whether local, cultural, political, etc. Anyone wishing to participate in this initiative, whether an individual or an organization, can send an email to: ice@humanistasrentabasica.org"

By allowing the audience to easily access a pathway for getting involved in the topic of the article, nonviolent journalism puts into practice the principle of *Beyond Information: Action.*

PRINCIPLES RELATED TO THE POINT OF VIEW OR THE LOOK

The point of view is always there

When we talk about *point of view,* we are referring to a particular way of looking at reality that conditions our interpretation of it and, therefore, our way of describing it. It is clear that there is no such thing as "objective communication." Our *look* is active.

Consciousness is not a hollow container that is filled from sensory impressions. A human being is not an automaton that records what the world presents to them without any processing. In every perception and representation made by the consciousness, it acts and modifies the signals that come from the external and internal worlds. If this were not the case, everyone would see the same thing, and this is obviously not the case.

As noted above, journalism, in any of its formats, always arises from a precondition that is determined by the journalist.

Even when a journalist considers the need for objectivity, they must recognise that this stance also stems from their own intention – conditioned by their personal situation, the place where they live and the historical time they live in – which they have chosen and applied to the task.

Immersed in the world, people are faced with the possibility of choosing different ways of looking at things. Thus, one of the few objective truths emerges: the subjective influence of the sender on what they communicate.

One's point of view can be rooted in a destructive or constructive direction. One can also choose to look the other way and let things take their course. In either case, the communicator's look is stamped on what they produce.

Let's take a simple example: a house. It will look very different when viewed from the outside or from the inside; from the front door or from the back; from the top floor of a nearby building or from the street. Depending on where it is viewed from, the impression will be quite different. We will always talk about the same house, but the stories will be astonishingly diverse. It should never be forgotten that there are many points of view regarding an object, an event, a place, etc., and as journalists we choose one of them.

As human beings, no matter how neutral we pretend to be, we have learned beliefs and values that affect our behaviour and even our physical sensations. This determines how we communicate. On top of this, there is the influence of the social environment in which we live, as well as the stance or editorial line of the media outlet we work for.

It is essential that, as communicators, we remember that we contribute to the construction of reality depending on how we position ourselves in relation to it, while it simultaneously transforms us. Everything is transformed, every person and the world in which they live, in a continuous interaction like a Moebius strip. This happens with or without our knowledge, regardless of our awareness of the filter through which we look and regardless of whether or not we decide to modify it.

In itself, this is neither good nor bad. It is a fact that needs to be understood in order to appreciate the importance and possible consequences of the stance we take.

Broadening the look and placing what we communicate in as broad a context as possible allows the audience to broaden their view of a news story.

In the framework of nonviolent journalism, we must ask ourselves whether what we narrate and how we narrate it generates violence of some kind or, on the contrary, enhances life; whether it contributes to the power of the few or to the empowerment of the many.

Every action has consequences whose end we do not know. Journalism is not exempt from this. In short, we must always bear in mind the point of view that conditions us, given our function in society as communicators.

Best Practice

Headline:	Syria and the Middle East: a violent approach to violence will not result in peace
Media:	Pressenza
Author:	Javier Tolcachier
Date:	April 30, 2012
Format:	Opinion piece
URL:	https://bit.ly/3ITM6sG

The author emphasises the importance of the point of view and highlights the complexity of the subject, its nuances, depending on the prism through which it is viewed. Even in the headline, it is clear that there is a difference in the approach and the angle from which the author tries to discover new aspects of the problem addressed. It also seeks to broaden the context by recognising the preceding historical process:

> *"With regard to the conflict in Syria and more broadly, in relation to the regional conflict in the Middle East, from a historical point of view, analysed over a broad period of time, it is necessary to consider the following:*

"The uprisings in the Arab world can in turn be understood as part of the process of deconstructing iron-fisted and repressive nation states, as an opening to a new moment. But at the same time, from a metahistorical point of view, they constitute a welcome juncture for the West in its attempt to regain the power it has lost over the region almost 1400 years ago.

"From a geopolitical point of view, in a look limited to shorter timescales, it is clear that in this destructuring, pan-Arabism and the search for greater freedoms are giving way to new Islamist currents of various hues."

Following an extensive analysis, the author identifies his own sensibility and point of view:

"Faced with this complex scenario, manipulated by the media, we express our opinion from our humanist perspective."

Headline:	Dismantling science's claim to neutrality
Media:	Desinformémonos
Author:	Eliana Gillet
Date:	October 27, 2015
Format:	Interview
URL:	https://bit.ly/38bi5YO

In this interview, it is clear where the subject of the interview will be speaking from.

In his profile, Argentinean researcher Horacio Machado Aráoz describes himself as someone who *"has always been linked to movements."* For the last 15 years he has been part of the resistance process against transnational open-cast mining as a member of the Sumak Kawsay Assembly in his native Catamarca. In this interview he talks about how this struggle has changed the way he practices and understands science.

The researcher comments on the installation of a mega-mining project in his province:

> *"We scientists began to work as neighbours in a process in which our territory was intervened upon without any kind of prior incident or informed consultation. That completely changed our perspective. We have always talked about critical science. One of its fundamental objectives is the deconstruction of science's supposed objectivity and neutrality. Science is not a form of knowledge detached from interests, positions and power structures. There is no such thing. The only way to do science is to make the interests that shape our research questions explicit.*

> *"There is a dispute over the manner in which truth is assigned. On the one hand we have a group of scientists working for the state or companies, who construct 'truths' to make these ventures viable.*

> *"The expropriation is not only geographical, material, of the mountain, the river or biodiversity, but also an epistemic expropriation, an expropriation of knowledge: they say 'these people don't know, they are not qualified to measure the impact and we are'. They don't care about the truth, about the validity of their knowledge, they are only interested in ensuring that the population's reaction does not affect the exploitation."*

The point of view expressed reveals the clash of interests around an issue involving knowledge and science, supposedly objective, unquestionable and neutral.

Human intentionality, the driving force of action

At the risk of repeating ourselves, the consciousness is active and far removed from the conception that considers people who communicate to be passive objects, as if they were information-transmitting machines. We are human beings with all that this implies, which leads us to go deeper into our conception of the human being that was the starting point of this book.

Human beings are intentional, which means that they have the capacity to transform the environment in which they live and to transform themselves. This is manifested in advances that accumulate and from which new generations benefit. Thus, with the proposals in this book we are trying to open paths for new steps of future communicators.

We once again recall the definition given by the founder of Universalist Humanism, Silo: *"Human beings are historical beings whose mode of social action transforms their own nature."* (Silo, 1996). We are part of and benefit from the historical process that has brought humanity this far. Our action transforms reality, at the same time as reality modifies us. As intentional beings, what we do has an impact on our personal and social future. Therefore, we must ask ourselves about the meaning of our action: why do we practise journalism? What are we looking for? And, why do we want to communicate what we are going to communicate? Who does it serve? And, for what purpose? If we keep in mind the meaning of our action, within our context, we will be able to decide what to cover and with which look. If we observe our work with a transcendent look, from the understanding that we are part of a process that precedes us and to which we can add for the benefit of other generations, then our actions will take on a depth that the greyness of everyday life and violence very often obscure.

Realising that we are intentional beings, capable of transforming ourselves and our environment from the field in which we work, allows us to understand that we work, together with other people who share our direction, for the future we aspire to. All this gives hope in the face of the despair that the media intentionally spreads today in an attempt to destroy any seed of utopia that proposes profound transformations based on necessity.

For communicators, the world has not only become smaller and more connected: it has also become larger, with access to a wider range of information sources. This, leaving aside the issue of monopolistic news agencies, makes for an improved horizon of choice. In turn, communicators are increasingly aware of the strength of their own information construction, of the power of their storytelling, of the energy they release in their critical and intentional vision.

As we said before, we are faced with the possibility of opting for different looks at things and with one truth: the subjective influence of the communicator on what they communicate.

We have commented, in general terms, on the option the communicator has to position themselves differently in a complex world where violence seems to be the prevalent – although not the only – form of relationship.

We know that there are other limitations on the freedom to communicate, stemming from the system in which journalism is entrenched. There is a dominant logic in the daily agenda, according to which, for example, any half-truth in the mouth of a well-known figure must be covered and repeated ad nauseam, instead of asking the opinions of those who genuinely delve into different issues. The barrier of commercial and political interests that expect to be compensated, because they finance the media, is patently obvious.

This is a major obstacle to the freedom to communicate: the political objectives pursued by many media, both private and public, whose editorial lines determine the content of what can or should be communicated. Despite this, there are communicators who choose a more evolutionary path, in other words, they contribute to a creative resolution of conflicts, to a perspective of nonviolence, and to a world to be humanised.

Best practice

Headline:	A humanising look at immigration is possible and urgent
Media:	Pressenza
Author:	Gabriela Amaya
Date:	November 25, 2016
Format:	Opinion piece
URL:	https://bit.ly/3LibGJA

The author draws on Juana Pérez Montero's analysis of the situation in which we find ourselves as communicators, through the phenomenon of migration, something which can be extrapolated to any other field:

"We conclude by stating that the media's role in the creation of the collective imagination means that they have an enormous responsibility with regards to the opinions that they hold on various issues; this is especially true of their views on migrants at this time."

In this case, Pressenza has intentionally chosen to work towards opening up the future, and the author has identified some useful elements for this purpose.

"At this exciting moment, which we can define as a critical crossroads, we are debating as humanity, as peoples, as individuals, between letting ourselves be carried away by fear; by resentment for what we have experienced or heard and incorporated

as our own; by revenge (the basis of the culture in which we live), or by opting for a new path: for a culture of dialogue, of understanding the phenomenon at its root, seeking personal and social reconciliation and demanding 'to treat others the way we would like to be treated,' an essential moral principle if we truly want to build a coexistence based on interculturality.

"At this crossroads — standing between looming disaster in an ever more violent and inhumane world, and the possibility of a new world based on peace and nonviolence — each of us will choose… and our actions will speak volumes.

"Pressenza is a collection of volunteer reporters — volunteers to avoid depending on outside interests — that has followed this second path since our founding. It is perhaps more accurate to say that we have found the need to create such a media organisation precisely because of our having chosen to follow this second path. Ours is an organisation that aims to serve the people, the grassroots, and the construction of a new paradigm worthy of humanity."

Headline:	Journalists as Historians of the Present
Media:	Pressenza
Author:	Juan Pablo Cárdenas Squella
Date:	December 6, 2020
Format:	Opinion piece
URL:	https://bit.ly/3wKHD9n

Chilean Juan Pablo Cárdenas Squella, winner of a National Prize for Journalism, analyses the role of the journalist and their essential position on what they communicate:

"If we go back to the founding and practice of our first schools of journalism, we can see that the ideal journalist was conceived as someone able to constrain themselves to the merely informative,

in other words, to make 'objectivity' their first and even only purpose... It was thought that a journalist should be objective, free from all judgement and prejudice, as if it were not in our own condition of gender, age, educational or social level to appreciate events in a different way, under our own optics and scale of values."

Further on, he gives his assessment of good journalism:

"We can be certain that all the great journalists we remember set out on a mission to change the world. On the other hand, we understand that the stars who always captivate on TV and the ratings-driven media are candles in the wind and unlikely to leave any legacy behind. Hence what is repeated within the same TV channels, that if a journalist decides to say something meaningful they should do so by writing a book."

Cárdenas names the beneficiaries of supposed neutrality:

"It is evident that communicators who seek to be neutral or objective end up giving us a vision of reality that is ultimately wrong or farcical. A caricature of the world taken over by big vested interests, leaders and, today, the billionaires who dominate the media and the powers of the state. There are those who even believe they are benefactors of journalism by performing the onerous task of publishing a newspaper; when in reality what they risk or lose in doing so is usually more than recouped in their collusion with the authorities and de facto powers they either represent or fear."

The author then recalls how certain professionals decided to take sides in the face of barbarism:

"After the long years of training to be 'sanitised' journalists who are only qualified to attend press conferences and reproduce as

literally as possible the opinions of their interviewees and events themselves has led many communicators to denounce and criticise the authorities and to adopt a strong commitment to the suffering, the discriminated and the abused. For many professionals, it became intolerable, of course, to observe reality and limit themselves to giving the official version of events and defending the position taken by their media company's owners.

"Human rights violations, for example, were the trigger in Chile and other countries for the emergence of so-called committed journalism. Willing to truly serve the great human cause of understanding and changing the world, as well as putting an end to flagrant injustices and abuses. Hence, with the Pinochet dictatorship, another of the most brilliant pages of journalism was opened and the will of numerous young journalists gave sustenance to the clandestine and dissident press that would contribute so much to the consciousness of the people, to their social mobilisation and legitimate insurrection.

"It is all the more absurd, then, that there are journalists and media outlets that aim to be objective, without serving as a sidekick or becoming accomplices of those who finance and manage them as instruments of their interests and privileges. They are committed to exercising a false neutrality that has no other purpose than to provoke the moral stupefaction of nations through the robotisation of intelligence and human behaviour."

Furthermore, he does not fail to draw attention to the situation of two people who are extremely committed to free access to information: Edward Snowden and Julian Assange.

"The incompatibility between good journalism and the interests of power has become clear in recent years with what has happened to Edward Snowden, a leading expert in computer security

since he decided to expose the secret spying operations of the National Security Agency (NSA) where he worked in the United States, after being a senior employee of the US Central Intelligence Agency (CIA).

"Convinced of the need to expose these illegitimate actions that even probed into the personal lives of a group of world leaders, supposedly allied to the government of his country. A task that has made Snowden one of the most wanted and persecuted human beings by his home country, forcing him to seek asylum in Russia.

"After several of the governments spied on by the United States thanked him for his invaluable revelation, they ultimately closed their borders to him in fear of affecting their countries' relationship with or dependence on the imperial power.

"Or the ordeal experienced by the Australian journalist Julian Assange, the founder of Wikileaks, who released a set of secret US files with the aim of 'preventing the powerful from continuing to exploit human beings around the world', as he warned. Well, Assange's chilling revelations, applauded from all over the world, were not enough to prevent him from receiving the subsequent slammed door in his face from many nations and governments, ending up in asylum in the Ecuadorian embassy in London and, now, trying to save himself from the slanderous accusations that have been brought before the English and Swedish courts in order to confine him for life or to send him to the United States, a country obsessed with his capture. Accusations that seek not to disprove what he revealed, of course, but to discredit him morally."

Responsibility vs. guilt

We live in a system that, to a large extent, relies on revenge and punishment as ways of compensating for harm done to communities and their members. To find where this comes from, we must go back some 4,000 years and look to the figure of Hammurabi and his code written on stelae of stone.

Since then, Western culture has been based on these principles. A clear example is in the field of law: someone commits a crime and they must pay for it. At the time, this approach was useful and a breakthrough in the face of vigilante justice.

This way of thinking, feeling and acting responds to a cultural construction. Understanding this allows us to denaturalise guilt, resentment and revenge, in order to question them and do better in the future.

Certain ways of conceiving human actions and relationships are based on the belief that an individual is completely free when they act and that they are not conditioned by history and society, which would make them guilty of their alleged harmful actions.

Guilt, a concept that we can find both in processes of community justice and in psychology, is closely related to the concept of debt, as proposed by Nietzsche in *The Genealogy of Morals*. (Nietzsche, 1887)

To explain this, he traces the development of the sense of justice in humanity.

Guilt carries a strong negative affective charge which our audience can easily identify with. From guilt is inferred – at least from certain parameters unfortunately still in force – the need for purging, punishment, flagellation, which, far from alleviating the problem, perpetuates and multiplies it.

Blaming does not automatically imply acknowledgement of the mistake. On the contrary, it often leads to public denial of what happened, defensiveness and deflection. This does not solve anything. The media's tendency to blame is often supported by the general public. It is a harmful mechanism, because it circumvents the responsibility of each individual to contribute to a better world.

This is not to say that there are no perpetrators and instigators of events. They do exist, but often they are not the ones who are usually singled out by the mechanisms of blame. Assigning responsibility is not the same as blaming. Responsibility points to actions or omissions, and indicates the need for a shared transformation that engages the entire community.

From the perspective of nonviolent journalism, shifting the focus from a discourse of blame to one of responsibility transforms the need for revenge or vengeance and puts the focus on the need for justice, understood as reparation and subsequent reconciliation which contributes to the re-establishment of social harmony.

It is therefore up to us, as communicators, to broaden our look once again and facilitate understanding of the context as well as the possible reasons behind the actions of those responsible for events, seeing any given situation as part of a wider process in order to open up the possibility for a restorative future.

For example, in a case of corruption, the aim would not be to stigmatise a specific person, but to highlight the systemic conditions inherent in the situation. Attacking the accused does not stop the cycle of corruption, but rather protects the system that produces it.

On the other hand, if we point out how political parties depend on large sums of money to finance their electoral campaigns and on the rewards they offer companies for their contributions, we can critically highlight one of the central conflicts of today's formal democracy. If, in addition, alternative horizons are proposed and alternative views of these practices are consulted, a significant public service will be provided and a path will be opened for everyone to understand and come to terms with their own shortcomings.

If we aspire to a better, humanised future, we need to lighten these negative charges in order to empower new paradigms, based on a culture of reconciliation and peace.[4]

Best Practice

Headline:	Collectives call for "I declare myself at peace" rally against those who say "we are at war".
Media:	teinteresa.es
Author:	Europa Press
Date:	November 25, 2016
Format:	Press release
URL:	https://bit.ly/36BsNYd

This article highlights the call to not take positions based on ideologies forged in the context of antagonistic factions, which necessarily reinforce confrontation and violence:

"In a statement, the organisers expressed their concern 'at the direction events are taking and the level of tension and fear to which people are being driven, seeking to position themselves on one side of the conflict'."

---

[4] In order to go deeper into this point, we recommend reading the interview with Luz Jahnen, producer of the documentary *Beyond Revenge* (Jahnen, 2016) conducted by Milena Rampoldi. (Rampoldi, 2015)

Furthermore, context is presented in order to understand the root of the problem, moving away from the dominant discourse that always blames the weaker party:

"Therefore, the conveners call for 'abandoning the path of revenge and seeking ways towards reconciliation. [...] We do not believe in the "defenders of good" who dedicate themselves to selling weapons, occupying territories, waging wars and bombing entire populations when their interests are opposed,' the statement adds."

Headline:	The Real Conflict
Media:	Pressenza
Author:	Javier Tolcachier
Date:	July 7, 2014
Format:	Opinion piece
URL:	https://bit.ly/3NE7jdF

The article refers to the killing of four young men in July 2014:

"One of them Palestinian. The other three Israelis. All belonging to the same generation, in the dawn of their lives. We know their faces. Thousands are no longer there, in Palestine, Syria, Iraq, Libya, Cambodia, Nicaragua, Guatemala, Vietnam, Algeria, Rwanda, Poland, Germany and Liberia. Faces gone without a trace. However, we carry all of them in our memory; and many others in so many other places without a name."

The author recalls the deaths of thousands of victims in various conflicts around the world, while at the same time looking at those responsible for such cruelty:

"Who will you blame for such crimes? The one who pulled the trigger? The one who manufactured the bullet and sold the gun? The one who inflamed the blood or sowed conflict with a speech? Tell me, please, who are you pointing your accusing finger at?

> *Those who, impassive in their palace weave – miserable in their wealth – the webs of pain for others? Those who invent stories to rob others and who care for nobody but themselves?"*

The article immediately highlights the futility of revenge, disguised as a claim for punishment or justice:

> *"Blaming without stating the context in which the atrocity is possible not only reveals short-sightedness, but makes one an accomplice of future sins by obscuring the roots of the conflict. Whoever demands punishment does not call for justice but seeks revenge. Does it repair the useless sacrifice of the victim? Does it mitigate the pain of the afflicted? Does it return the beloved to life? Does it prevent a future genocide? Or rather, does it feed it?"*

Further on, the article points to certain urgent horizons:

> *"The people must unite and understand the futility of continuing the confrontation.*

> *"The real conflict is between remaining hostages to opposing factions in the discourse, but united in the destructive action, or to rebel and refuse to support any of these factions. It is between those who believe that self-interest or one's own worldview is sufficient justification to impose on others, and on many of us who cherish human freedom and diversity of life. It is between those who profit from war, those who want to maintain their power and possessions against the needs of the world's dispossessed, those majorities in daily struggle to build a dignified existence."*

Finally, the author emphatically affirms the need to take the side of reconciliation:

"We are all responsible for seeking and finding reconciliation with those who have hurt us and for repairing our own mistakes. If instead, we wield justifications to continue endorsing the inexcusable, we are cooperating only with the growing spiral of violence, just drawing away the possibility of a different future, locking ourselves between the walls of prehistory."

The wealth of diversity

Nonviolent journalism implies a deep respect and intentional search for diverse sources, points of view about, and aspects of, what we want to say, distancing ourselves from discrimination and rejecting complicity in the silencing to which the majority of the population is subjected.

This position distances us from the homogenisation of the dominant discourse, which self-interestedly seeks to impose a single narrative in order to maintain control over the people.

On the other hand, time and time again we see how information is reduced to sound bites; how it is oversimplified, trivialised and pushed towards polarisation; how it reinforces confrontation, the lack of arguments and the reductionism of contexts. This impoverishes us as societies while those in power rub their hands together in glee.

It is absolutely necessary to show different sides of the story, to show the roots of the issue, the process of the news. In the cultural field, it is essential to recognise different cultures and their different ways of understanding and acting in the world. This allows a change of perspective and the recognition of narratives that escape the dominant Western discourse.

Advocating for multiplicity of sources, showing cultural diversity, broadening perspectives, approaching other protagonists and giving voice to the grassroots dilute prejudices and encourage solidarity, creativity and responsiveness as a community, bringing out the best in all of us. This makes us smarter as a whole and undoubtedly freer as individuals and as a society.

Finally, we cannot forget one fundamental aspect: the search for nonviolent, collaborative experiences, projects and ways of living, which project us towards a new world which most people aspire to. We need to publish stories that are signs of that world, stories that exist but that go unnoticed because they are not of interest to the violent official discourse.

In a scenario of increasing globalisation, it is essential to give space to and revalue the contributions of different cultures, their activities, experiences, lifestyles and knowledge, thus contributing to surpassing cultural hegemony and building paths towards other futures.

Best practice

Headline:	Ouaga Girls, a small African revolution
Media:	Afroféminas
Author:	Afroféminas
Date:	February 3, 2019
Format:	News report
URL:	https://bit.ly/3qPETDR

In this article you will find different elements that illustrate the defence of diversity that we advocate:

"The Ouaga Girls decided not to live in silent, passive resignation and took the initiative.

"For this reason, two years ago, Honorine and her friends enrolled in a vocational school that is part of a social development

project funded by the African Economic Community. Since the late 1990s, many girls have chosen to study at the CFIAM, an educational centre for the initiation and teaching of trades to women. The car repair sector is a field largely reserved for men, but Bintou, Chantale and Dina, like many of their peers, decided to bring down the gender barrier and become professional mechanics. The rest is a story that unfolds among screwdrivers, spanners and rusty engines in a sector of a profession associated with masculinity. A gender barrier that has not discouraged them."

Rebellion against the status quo and the value of collaborative work are highlighted:

"Ouaga Girls is a story about life choices, friendship and the effort it takes to find your own way. Through this group of female mechanics, director Theresa Traoré Dahlberg brings us closer to the inevitable and universally difficult transition from adolescence to adulthood. A poetic description of what it means to be a young woman today in Burkina Faso. A small African revolution."

Headline:	Brooklyn Heights Interfaith Clergy Association Response to Anti-Semitic Violence in our Region
Media:	Pressenza
Author:	Pressenza New York
Date:	February 3, 2019
Format:	News report
URL:	https://bit.ly/3iOBXTo

In a materialistic world that looks with suspicion at non-hegemonic religious manifestations, giving space to diverse religions is fundamental. In addition, this article highlights the richness generated by collective work between diverse actors and highlights their joint commitment in the face of violence:

"The Brooklyn Heights Interfaith Clergy Association is composed of neighbourhood imams, ministers, pastors, priests, and rabbis who have gathered once a month for decades to represent thousands of faithful neighbours at the table.

"As a multi-faith group we affirm that every person is made in the divine image and possesses inherent dignity and worth. We are enriched by the spirituality of one another's traditions and impoverished when any member of our community is threatened or diminished.

"We are hurt and sickened by recent attacks on Jewish people in our region. Attacks on visibly religious people are attacks on religious life, itself. Anti-Semitism is an expression of evil and a crime against the human family.

"The Brooklyn Heights Interfaith Clergy Association values religious diversity and interfaith bonds. We support our Jewish brothers and sisters in the face of anti-Semitism and at all times.

"We invite those who fear our differences to embrace the joy of diversity and join us in peace."

Headline:	Historic decriminalisation of homosexuality in India
Media:	El Espectador
Author:	El Espectador
Date:	September 6, 2018
Format:	News report
URL:	https://bit.ly/3NAzOcl

When dealing with diversity, a deep respect for it is essential. For example, it is essential to take into account the historical progress made with regard to LGBTQI+ rights in different parts of the world.

This article in *El Espectador* reports on what has happened in India, the second most populous country on the planet, which after a long period of resistance has recognised the rights of this group:

"The fight for equal rights for the LGBT community won a historic battle on Thursday with the decriminalisation of homosexuality by the Supreme Court of India, the world's second most populous nation. The highest court in the South Asian country of 1.25 billion people ruled unconstitutional a long-standing article condemning same-sex sexual relations.

"This provision 'had become a weapon of harassment against the LGBT community,' said Chief Justice Dipak Misra. Under the Indian penal code, which dates back to the British colonial era, homosexuality was punishable by up to life imprisonment. But in fact, convictions for same-sex relationships were very rare."

It echoes the initial thoughts of the people at the centre of the story, by obtaining an on-the-spot reaction:

"'I am stunned! It took a long time to come, but at last I can say that I am free and have the same rights as everyone else,' enthused Rama Vij, a student from Kolkata, who gathered with friends to follow the reading of the ruling in front of the television."

In addition, some of the international reaction to this issue is reflected in the report:

"India thus becomes the 124th country in the world where homosexual acts are not – or are no longer – criminalised, according to the International Lesbian, Gay, Bisexual, Trans and Intersex Association."

New sensibilities in the contemporary world

The journalistic approach that we propose places great value on context and history. This makes it essential to situate oneself in the period and, from there, to observe where events arise and what the emerging sensibilities are that, from their particularities, advance with nonviolent forms towards the humanisation of our societies.

Each era brings new subjects, faces and feelings. People made invisible in previous times emerge and fight for their space within societies and as historical subjects. This is what happened with the women who fought for their right to vote and then never stopped. Likewise, hundreds of communities have reclaimed their narratives and have put them into circulation, such as the indigenous and black populations, who were systematically hidden until they themselves acquired resources and appropriated spaces.

The same has happened to children, youth, LGBTIQ+ people and many other marginalised majorities, hidden behind monolithic, racist, white, patriarchal discourse.

Seeing the world in which we live and to which we relate in a structural way means, among many other things; learning to see where new sensibilities are; understanding their looks and narratives in the context we live in; and, detecting that this is not just discourse or appearance but is, in reality, a new way of feeling and experiencing life.

The looks, the stories, the ways of feeling and experiencing that emerge from feminisms, ecologies, young and multiple aesthetics bring with them innovative readings and alternatives. The same happens with the ancestral memory expressed in the proposals for caring for life, which come from centuries of wisdom and at the same time bring with them unprecedented alternatives.

It is crucial to remember that the new – in terms of sensibility – is not defined by its years of existence, but by its questioning of the establishment and the changes of look it proposes.

In this immense field of new sensibilities to be identified, we seek to make visible those who demand life, freedom, the right to be, dignity, and who do so through nonviolent means. This is the task of journalism, today, on the road to a new future.

Those who are part of these new sensibilities are not only part of the story, because those who tell the story modify their point of view and generate new ways of practising the craft:

"We are committed to those forms of journalism that are born in virtual and physical communities and come together in our investigations to talk about identities. We accept the risks involved with battling against speculation, ignorance, simplification and silence. We reclaim ethical conduct as the meaning of the profession, and we urge explicit commitment to stories that are urban, black, rural, indigenous, regarding old age, sexuality, youth, religion, women, and others; and to development from the deepest of human aspirations." (Acosta Damas, 2017)

Best practice

Headline:	More than 200 young people gathered for the VI International Conference of La Vía Campesina
Media:	La Vía Campesina
Author:	La Vía Campesina Press Team
Date:	June 10, 2013
Format:	Feature story
URL:	https://bit.ly/3qNnr2M

The article highlights the protagonism of young people within a long-standing international movement; the new generations taking up the baton of historical struggles from their own sensibility:

"The third International Youth Assembly of La Vía Campesina began on Saturday in Jakarta, capital of Indonesia, with a mystical activity and speeches by members of the movement and invited guests.

"'In the strength of the youth of La Vía Campesina lies also the responsibility to advance in the construction of our movement, in the struggles and resistances of the peoples. For food sovereignty, the youth of La Vía Campesina in struggle.' So Juana Ferrer, from the National Confederation of Peasant Women of the Dominican Republic (CONAMUCA), closed her brief opening presentation today."

"In this process of building La Vía Campesina, youth have taken up the challenge to derail capitalism, patriarchy and its neoliberal politics. The struggle, resistance and commitment of La Vía Campesina's youth is growing deeper and deeper."

Headline:	Hackfeminisms to confront colonial, capitalist and heteropatriarchal domination on the Internet
Media:	Internet Ciudadana
Author:	Communication Forum for the Integration of OurAmerica
Date:	September 23, 2020
Format:	Feature story
URL:	https://bit.ly/3Nvcf4y

This feature story brings together the central ideas put forward by three feminist women from different countries in Latin America and the Caribbean, who campaign as hackers and for a free, open and secure internet. The convergence of feminist sensibilities in the world of technology is made visible:

"What is hackfeminism? What is the impact of 5G networks on women and diversities? How to decolonise and depatriarchalise a technology built by white men from the North? How to address

the care of women, children and diversities in the network? What are futurotopias? How to sustain community and feminist infrastructures?

"Loreto Bravo, from Mexico, from the Digital Defenders Partnership's Digital Security Accompaniment programme; from Ecuador, Anais Córdova-Páez from the organisation Women's Communication Workshop, in charge of the programme Navigating Free on the Net; and Colombian Tatiana Avendaño, transhackfeminist philosopher, raver, digital security practitioner and apprentice of telepathy and clairvoyance, were invited to speak on the topics.

Aspects of Loreto Bravo's intervention are highlighted:

"[...] companies are selling us the idea of hyper-connectivity through fifth generation networks (5G) and the Internet of Things, crossing the personal-intimate boundary and invading our bodies and minds. In relation to women's bodies, 'this is worrying because it allows men, who largely develop and market these technologies, to access new "data," feeding their algorithms with women's emotions, psychological states and biorhythms' [...] She added that an important challenge we have as a society is to understand that the companies that dominate the design and development of the digital technologies that today build this new reality are directly linked to a colonial, capitalist and heteropatriarchal logic."

In addition, emphasis is placed on gender-based violence in the digital sphere:

"Anais Córdova-Páez said that 'gender violence in the digital sphere is a form of discrimination, harassment, exploitation,

*abuse and aggression that occurs through the use of social net-
works, email, mobile phones and any medium within the information and communication technologies (ICTs), which entails
different physical, psychological, sexual and economic effects'
[...] She added that 'technologies must be comfortable, safe
spaces for us to inhabit. Moreover, technologies must be made,
designed by us, based on our needs, in other words, feminist
technology'."*

The article also takes up other meanings of hackfeminism and closes
with a projection into possible futures:

*"Tatiana Avendaño unveiled the meaning of transhackfeminism:
trans, as a reference to transformation, transgression and tran-
sience; hack, in the sense of producing something new, turning
something upside down to use it in a different way. We can and
know how to hack not only technology, but also bodies, laws,
things, markets, patterns of behaviour.'*

*"Futurotopias, she said, are an invitation to confront speculative
practices and images with social and feminist politics, joyful actions and radical tenderness, 'a world that seems to be going
from bad to worse, where the options, images and futures that
are proposed to us oscillate more and more between cynicism
and dystopia'.*

*"These are political tools that 'historically have allowed femi-
nisms to imagine the world we want to live in, because the current models are exhausted and loaded with patriarchy'."*

PRINCIPLES RELATED TO VIOLENCE AND NONVIOLENCE

The unacceptability of violence in any of its forms

In the opening pages of this book, we defined violence as any attempt to deny the intention of another person, thus denying our own human condition. We assert that violence is not part of a supposed *human nature*, even though this is proclaimed from deep-rooted beliefs. Such beliefs constitute prejudice against the proposal of nonviolent journalism: if violence is part of our nature, what is the point of nonviolence or journalism based on it?

On the contrary, we argue that the human species is in a process of constant transformation. Part of this process is precisely the overcoming of violence. Violence is not an automatic consequence of conflict and, as Galtung says, human beings always have the possibility of responding from their *"capacity for peace"*.

This principle of our journalistic approach stems from these assertions. Violence is anti-human and dehumanising.

From our journalistic work, we seek to contribute to overcoming it. Any kind of violence is unacceptable.

The unacceptability of any form of violence (economic, racial, religious, cultural, physical, psychological, symbolic, etc.) is not synonymous with denial: violence exists and must be exposed to its very roots, as will be seen below.

This principle of unacceptability of violence demands not justifying it. Although it is necessary to analyse the geographical and historical context in which violence takes place, as well as its goals, interests and positions, this analysis does not imply justification, and even less acceptance. Strictly speaking, it is the opposite. Analysis is the question of why, the search for causes, the contribution to understanding the origins, forms and consequences. We are talking about a contribution – from the journalistic practices of information gathering and investigation – to the overcoming and elimination of the multiple expressions of violence.

Paraphrasing Galtung, whereas direct violence is visible, structural and cultural violence are invisible, but they are both intimately related to direct violence. If we don't understand this, we can't move forward in the search for peace. (Galtung, 1990)

Best practice

Headline:	London Demo: 'Stop Arming Israel, Stop Bombing Gaza'
Media:	Common Dreams
Author:	Jake Johnson
Date:	May 13, 2019
Format:	Feature story
URL:	https://bit.ly/3tYKauX

This feature story reports on a march held in London, condemning the violence suffered by the Palestinian people and denouncing the Israeli occupation. At the same time, it highlights the complicity of corporations and the UK government in demanding an end to arms sales to the oppressive government of Israel.

The then leader of the Labour party, Jeremy Corbyn, is quoted:

> *"'We cannot stand by or stay silent at the continuing denial of rights and justice to the Palestinian people,' Corbyn wrote. 'The silence of many governments, including our own, has been deafening. The U.K. government should instead unequivocally con-*

demn the killing of demonstrators – including children, paramedics, and journalists – and other civilians, and freeze arms sales to Israel'."

Headline:	Hunger will kill us before coronavirus does
Media:	Tricontinental Institute for Social Research
Author:	Vijay Prashad
Date:	September 24, 2020
Format:	Opinion piece
URL:	https://bit.ly/3iSdHQz

The article opens as follows:

"In April 2020, a month after the World Health Organisation (WHO) declared the pandemic, the UN's World Food Programme (WFP) warned that the numbers of people who lived with acute hunger around the world would double due to COVID-19 by the end of 2020 'unless swift action is taken'."

One paragraph later, it points out the lack of media visibility given to the real perpetrators of this unacceptable havoc:

"None of these reports made the front pages of newspapers. Little was made of the fact that this is not a crisis of food production – since we have enough food in the world to feed everyone – but a crisis of social inequality."

FAO Director-General Qu Dongyu is quoted as warning of, *"'looming famine' in many parts of the world, particularly in Burkina Faso, South Sudan, and Yemen. It is now estimated that one in two people on the planet struggles with hunger. No-one should go to bed hungry at night."*

The article also refers to wars as drivers of devastation, death, disease and famine:

> *"Yemen, which has faced an unyielding war prosecuted by Saudi Arabia and the United Arab Emirates (backed fully by the West and by arms manufacturers), has struggled with famine and with desert locusts and now with the enormity of the pandemic. Two days after Qu made these comments, UN Secretary General António Guterres pleaded for an end to the war on Yemen. The war had 'decimated the country's health facilities', Guterres said, which are not able to tackle the near million cases of COVID-19 in the country. The war, he said, has 'devastated the lives of tens of millions of Yemenis'."*

The piece delves into the systemic irrationality that generates hunger, using the example of the Democratic Republic of Congo:

> *"The famine sweeping these countries is not for want of resources. The DRC has 80 million acres of arable land, which could feed two billion people if it were cultivated with food crops in an agro-ecological manner; but, as of now, only 10% of the country's arable land is cultivated. Meanwhile, the country spends $1.5 billion per year in food imports – money that could be used to invest in the agricultural sector, where the main work is done by women subsistence farmers (who own less than 3% of the cultivated land). A lack of power amongst the agricultural workers and the farmers results in a lopsided system that privileges a handful of agri-business conglomerates rather than cooperatives and family farms."*

After reviewing similar situations in India and other countries, the article condemns violence against those who want to work the land in a just way, stressing the need to democratise land ownership and create autonomous projects with self-sustainable farming technologies:

> *"As hunger increases, so does the attack on those who farm the soil. Little wonder that farmers and agricultural workers across*

India say that hunger will kill them before coronavirus. This is a slogan familiar to farmers and agricultural workers from Brazil, who – as we demonstrate in our dossier no. 27 Popular Agrarian Reform and the Struggle for Land in Brazil – have long been in the midst of a fight to bring democracy to the land. Like Sankara's Burkina Faso, the brave sem terras [landless] of Brazil have their own project: to reforest land that was once saturated with agro-toxins, to occupy unused land that they then farm through agro-ecological practices, and to forge 'a broad demand for a new vision for the country as a whole'."

Denouncing systemic oppression

Our social organisation is characterised by violence. The concentration of power in the hands of a few and the unequal access to resources essential for people's survival and development place humanity in a framework of systemic violence. The current scale of values, with money at the top, sustains a materialist system that denies equal rights and opportunities for all of humanity.

Nonviolent journalism therefore has a dual function: to point out the contexts of systemic violence that frame current events and to report on the perspectives that have emerged to address injustice.

In any given situation, it is possible to critically examine the elements that trap the human race in a spiral of violence and, on the other hand, those that enable its growing liberation.

This journalistic approach observes societies and human beings in a permanent dynamic. Therefore, it considers that every historical period, every system and every belief tends towards self-perpetuation, tends to conserve what has been consolidated, without giving way to the new. Although there are forms of social organisation that favour a nonviolent human relationship, their crystallisation is usually limited by the imposition of particular interests. Thus, a fundamental journalistic duty is to dynamise the way of looking at things in order to facilitate the opening up of new historical moments.

Oppression ignores the evolutionary imperative of human beings, who always seek to modify their environment towards new horizons of possibility. At the same time, the aggressive desire for conservation makes it difficult for existing social orders to recognise the impact of generational renewal. This is why giving space to the transformative irruption of new generations is also a key element of our journalistic approach.

Nonviolent journalism opens up space for the critical expression of new emerging sensibilities and resolutely opposes historical paralysis.

Best practice

Headline:	Egypt: The merry race to the abyss: Why does the West support the Sissi regime?
Media:	Sin Permiso
Author:	Hipatia Urabi
Date:	December 19, 2020
Format:	Opinion piece
URL:	https://bit.ly/3K3aTfl

The article analyses the deterioration in the quality of life of the Egyptian people and the setbacks since the democratic reforms achieved by the revolution of 2011. Similarly, based on the Amnesty International report for 2019 (Amnesty International, 2020), it denounces the repressive nature of the regime:

> *"The authorities have deployed a range of repressive measures against protesters or perceived opponents, particularly after the 20 September anti-presidential demonstrations. Enforced disappearances, mass arrests, torture and ill-treatment, excessive use*

of force and harsh evidentiary measures appear to be widely employed. The security forces have arbitrarily arrested and imprisoned at least 20 journalists for the sole reason of peacefully expressing their opinions."

With typical Egyptian humour, the article uses irony to criticise the degradation of democracy.

"Sissi has announced on several occasions that he only wanted to stay in power for two terms, but he has been very surprised by the population's strong desire for him to remain in power and, of course, he had to obey the will of the people. In this theatre of the absurd, Egyptians use their most powerful weapon: humour. Sadly, this is of no help to them in their misfortune."

Finally, it highlights the structural condition of the violence faced, linking the permanence of this situation to the interests of international banks:

"Egypt clearly relies on debt to create forms of financial dependency between the regime and international partners. The regime has borrowed huge sums of money.

"The regime's transformation into a major arms importer has two main consequences for the oppression of the Egyptian people by their regime and the futility of international humanitarian efforts to democratise Egypt.

"Firstly, the close linkage and responsibility of Western countries and their arms industry, as the main supplier of surveillance and mass control, in the repression of popular movements;

"Secondly, the potential for Western countries to condemn and address human rights violations is thus automatically eliminated."

The article is based on a large amount of data, constituting an excellent example of critical journalism and denunciation of the systemic violence in a country.

Headline:	Uprising & Abolition: Angela Davis on Movement Building, "Defund the Police" & Where We Go from Here
Media:	Democracy Now
Author:	Amy Goodman
Date:	June 12, 2020
Format:	Interview
URL:	https://bit.ly/3K3Llig

This interview appears in the context of the uprising against police violence and racism that began after the death of George Floyd at the hands of police in Minneapolis on 25 May 2020 which *"dramatically shifted public opinion on policing and systemic racism, as 'defund the police' becomes a rallying cry of the movement."*

In this introduction, the violent structural nature of racism and the actions of the US police against African-Americans are described. It also points to a novel, nonviolent way out of the conflict: *Defund the Police*:

> *"This is an extraordinary moment. I have never experienced anything like the conditions we are currently experiencing, the conjuncture created by the COVID-19 pandemic and the recognition of the systemic racism that has been rendered visible under these conditions because of the disproportionate deaths in Black and Latinx communities. And this is a moment I don't know whether I ever expected to experience.*

> *"When the protests began, of course, around the murder of George Floyd and Breonna Taylor and Ahmaud Arbery and Tony McDade and many others who have lost their lives to racist state violence and vigilante violence – when these protests erupted, I*

remembered something that I've said many times to encourage activists, who often feel that the work that they do is not leading to tangible results. I often ask them to consider the very long trajectory of Black struggles. And what has been most important is the forging of legacies, the new arenas of struggle that can be handed down to younger generations."

The guest gives a clear demonstration of a nonviolent struggle to overcome systemic conditions of violence, with clearly defined horizons:

"Defunding the police is not simply about withdrawing funding for law enforcement and doing nothing else. […] It's about shifting public funds to new services and new institutions – mental health counsellors, who can respond to people who are in crisis without arms. It's about shifting funding to education, to housing, to recreation. All of these things help to create security and safety. It's about learning that safety, safeguarded by violence, is not really safety.

"And I would say that abolition is not primarily a negative strategy. It's not primarily about dismantling, getting rid of, but it's about re-envisioning. It's about building anew. And I would argue that abolition is a feminist strategy. And one sees in these abolitionist demands that are emerging the pivotal influence of feminist theories and practices."

Prioritising nonviolent conflict resolution

It is clear that our proposed journalistic approach seeks out, makes visible and highlights those processes that aim to resolve conflicts in a nonviolent way, in any sphere of life in our societies. We consider it a priority to identify and open space for proposals for dialogue, mediation, rapprochement and negotiation in any part of the world.

But, how can journalism contribute to identifying, prioritising and strengthening nonviolent solutions? In their book, *Reporting Conflict: new directions in peace journalism,* Lynch and Galtung, contrast war journalism with peace journalism and elaborate a table of characteristics of peace journalism which is full of useful considerations. For Lynch and Galtung, peace journalism is:

Conflict-solution-oriented

- *Exploring the various elements of a conflict: all the parties involved, their different goals, and the general issues. Looking for win-win solutions*
- *Providing historical and cultural context for a conflict which clearly did not appear fully fledged on the first day that physical violence erupted*
- *Focusing on the invisible effects of violence, such as the psychological damage to the population*
- *Reporting transparently*
- *Giving voices to all parties*
- *Focusing on creativity*
- *Humanising all sides*
- *Starting to report before a looming conflict turns into physical violence and death*

Truth-oriented

- *Exposing lies on all sides*
- *Uncovering all the cover-ups*

People-oriented

- *Reporting the violence and suffering of all sides*
- *Reporting the experiences of all sectors of civil society (women, young, old, minorities of all kinds)*

- *Naming those responsible*
- *Focusing on those working towards peace*

Solution-oriented

- *Showing that peace = nonviolence + creativity*
- *Highlighting peace initiatives*
- *Looking at the structural and cultural roots of the conflict in order to identify structural and cultural changes*
- *Giving space to reconciliation and reconstruction. (Lynch & Galtung, 2010, pp. 12-14)*

There is one central idea that traverses nonviolent conflict resolution: in the midst of any conflict, there are always human beings. This is something we must never forget in our journalistic practice.

Best practice

Headline:	South Sudan at a crossroads
Media:	LolaMora Productions
Author:	Blanca Diego
Date:	May 25, 2014
Format:	Opinion piece
URL:	https://bit.ly/37giacY

The article clearly shows who the victims of the war are and establishes responsibilities. It also identifies the actors working for peace and highlights the damage to the civilian population:

"It is not all the states that make up South Sudan, nor is it all the people of South Sudan that are suffering from the war, but the rivalry between the two historic great men – representing two great tribes – from the struggle for the independence of the Islamic Republic of Sudan is the reason why the country has been paralysed and plunged into such a catastrophe.

"In an interview on BBC World's HardTalk programme on 19 May, the President of the Republic, Salva Kiir Mayardit, a Dinka, evaded direct responsibility for the violence that broke out last December in Juba, and pointed the finger at his opponent, the Nuer, former deputy prime minister, Riek Machar. Salva Kiir admitted in the interview that there will be famine if the war does not stop and that he will not leave office before elections are held. The Nuer and Dinka — the two most powerful and populous tribes — entered last December into a spiral of attacks and counter-attacks where killings are avenged in equally violent acts.

"The African Union, the Inter-American Commission on Human Rights, Amnesty International and the United Nations are conducting investigations to establish accountability for human rights violations and war crimes committed.

"The statistics, always cold and abstract, scarcely give an idea of the tragedy that Africa's youngest country is going through. But it is a fact that since last February, the height of the conflict, the situation has only worsened. 3.5 million people are dependent on external aid and a million are no longer living at home but in the open, in camps set up for temporary shelter or in neighbouring countries.

"Cholera, against which thousands of vaccines were administered between February and April, has been unstoppable and is already claiming lives in the capital; some schools have closed. Outside Juba, having seeds and being able to keep livestock alive are critical to the survival of families and groups, so under the temporary cessation of hostilities, the UN World Food Programme (FAO) is distributing basic aid packages. The UN Office for the Coordination of Humanitarian Affairs (OCHA) says that by December, 1 in every 2 South Sudanese will be directly affected by the war.

"On the 20th of this month, in order to reverse the apathy and neglect, a conference of donor countries took place in Norway. They have pledged 600 million dollars; more than a billion dollars is needed, according to the UN.

"On 23 January, the Agreement on Cessation of Hostilities signed in Addis Ababa promised an end to the conflict one month after it began. It was an empty promise, ignored by both factions. In fact, the bloodiest weeks began thereafter. At least three major South Sudanese cities are now ashes and rubble: Bentiu, Malakal and Bor. Between February and April, the Nuer and Dinka looted, burned, robbed and killed. Children were recruited as combatants, girls and women were raped and young women were abducted (an ancestral practice among several clans and tribes in the country).

"The gradual agreements reached at the negotiating table, set up since January in the Ethiopian capital and sponsored by the Intergovernmental Authority on Development (IGAD), have at their core the recognition that there is no military solution to this crisis and that lasting peace can only be achieved through dialogue. The gulf between rhetoric and action is huge.

"For the time being, the two leaders are holding a shaky one-month truce, which has already been disregarded and which they signed with barely a word to each other. This cessation of hostilities will allow for the delivery of food, seeds and other essentials. The Dinka-Nuer standoff is not the only one.

"Between 2012 and 2013, in Greater Pibor County, Jonglei State, the Murle – another of the country's ethnic groups – rebelled against the central government of Salva Kiir to demand basic services, political rights and greater administrative autonomy. The clashes resulted in many deaths and the use of violence against

the civilian population. This conflict was resolved with the signing of a peace agreement a few weeks ago. And so, since 2011, when the new African state was created, there have been other inter-communal conflicts, sometimes on a smaller scale, but almost always violent and resulting in death, destruction and open wounds that will one day, at some point, be avenged."

The alternatives for dialogue are emphasised, as well as the importance of nonviolent conflict resolution:

"In a recent article, Canadian anthropologist Carol Berger detailed the background to the violence in South Sudan. Berger says that anyone attempting to answer the question of whether there will be individual responsibility for crimes committed in the country should know that 'responsibility for the death of others is communal (collective) in nature and is a norm throughout the country.' Carol Berger, who has lived for years in the South Sudanese town of Rumbek, explains that the act perpetrated by one individual is in reality seen as an act committed by all those associated with that individual. According to Berger, to say that the December war broke out because of a power struggle between President Salva Kiir and former Vice President Riek Machar is to misunderstand the nature of the military political system of the two dominant cultural groups, the Dinka and the Nuer. The two groups will resume political negotiations in June in Addis Ababa, with the presence of civil society, churches and regional allies. One of the main points agreed is the installation of 'a transitional government of national unity' leading to elections. Neither Machar nor Kiir seem willing to relinquish power; a transitional government without them is desirable but impossible. The country's peace and security will again be discussed around a diplomatic table, but it is Kiir and Machar – Dinka and Nuer – who

have the last word because they are the ones who put the rest of the country on the precipice."

Headline:	Are we Heading Toward WWIII & Nuclear War?
Media:	In Depth News
Author:	Alice Slater
Date:	March 17, 2022
Format:	Opinion piece
URL:	https://rb.gy/4ktczu

The saying, "truth is the first casualty in war," is often attributed to the US Senator Hiram Warren Johnson in 1918 and there are variations on it that stretch back throughout history including this one from the Ancient Greek philosopher, Aeschlyus who said, "God is not averse to deceit in a just cause"!

The first thing that a warring party does is impose control over the media where this is not already the case. In Western countries that label themselves as democracies, one might think that control over an "independent" media would be impossible to achieve. However, it doesn't take much investigation to discover that a dozen or so unelected and unaccountable billionaires control enormous swathes of the West's media landscape. People such as Rupert Murdoch, Michael Bloomberg and Jeff Bezos among others ensure that public opinion stays in line with their personal priorities rather than the priorities that humanity as a whole would choose. Whether the billionaires and oligarchs live in the West, Russia, China, Iran or Saudi Arabia, control of the media is overwhelmingly in their hands.

Thus the task of nonviolent journalism is to give space to those who aren't promoting war as a means to resolve conflict.

In this article by a long-time peace campaigner from New York, the author takes a conflict-solution-oriented approach simply by providing elements for a different narrative. She starts out by criticising the mainstream media.

"It has become unbearable to observe the Western media, in the grip of corrupt military contractors, wielding their undue influence on the unknowing victims of the media "news" reports as they publicly and shamelessly celebrate their enormous profits this year from the billions of dollars in weapons they are selling to keep the Ukraine war going.

"The drumbeat of demonization and excoriation of Putin by the western media, as the sole provocative cause of all the current havoc and evil, with hardly a word devoted to the historical context that brought us to this tragic turn of events is unconscionable."

The author then takes up one of Lynch and Galtung's points by providing historical and cultural context for the conflict.

"There is barely any reporting in the Western press of the events leading up to this violence, resulting from the corrupt path the western neoliberal corporate corrupters followed, ever since the blessed ending of the Cold War when Gorbachev ended the Soviet occupation, dissolving the Warsaw Pact, without a shot.

"The US promised him, in a host of documents and testimonies that are surfacing recently, including from Reagan's Ambassador Jack Matlock, that if Russia didn't object to a unified Germany joining NATO, it would not expand one inch to the East.

"Since Russia lost 27 million people to the Nazi onslaught, they had good reason to be fearful of an expanded western military alliance."

Some historical data is provided to highlight US hypocrisy:

"Yet the arrogance of the United States has been breath-taking over these years. Not only did the US expand NATO taking in 14 countries from Poland to Montenegro, it bombed Kosovo over Russia's Security Council objection, breaking its treaty obligation with the UN never to commit a war of aggression without Security Council approval unless under imminent threat of attack, which was certainly not the case with Kosovo.

"Further, it walked out of the 1972 Anti-Ballistic Missile Treaty, left the Intermediate Nuclear Forces Treaty as well as the carefully negotiated deal with Iran to preclude their enriching uranium to bomb grade. Shockingly, the US keeps nuclear weapons in five NATO states: Germany, Belgium, the Netherlands, Italy, and Turkey."

The author humanises citizens of the other faction and prods us to look in the sinister direction of where events are leading.

"The current media drumbeat for war, the glee expressed by reporters and commentators at the prospect of all the devastating economic sanctions we are inflicting on the Russian people, in retribution for what they describe as Putin's provocative invasion of Ukraine, and the constant drumbeat of how evil and crazy Putin is, may indeed be putting us on the path to World War and nuclear war at that."

Finally, the author proposes nonviolent measures that focus on human security.

"Let Ukraine agree to be neutral like Finland and Austria instead of insisting they have a right to be part of our military alliance which Putin has been pleading with us for years to stop expanding.

> *"It was perfectly reasonable for Putin to require that Ukraine not become a member of NATO and we should take him up on it and save the world from the scourge of war with new programs of cooperation to end the plague [COVID-19], abolish nuclear weapons, and save our Mother Earth from looming catastrophic climate destruction."*

Tackling conflict and violence from an ethic of non-violence

Approaching communication from a perspective of nonviolence does not mean distorting, denying events or propagating idyllic perspectives free from conflicting meanings. How can violence, conflict and criticism be tackled from this journalistic look? Violence, conflict and criticism, far from being excluded, are important topics for nonviolent journalism.

The general context in which our raw material is framed is marked by an essentially violent system of values. This characterisation is based on the fact that human dignity, equal rights and opportunities, the guarantee of survival, care and compassion are relegated by anti-values such as money, unbridled consumption, appropriation, competition and the degradation of others.

This leads some human beings to see their fellow human beings as objects which favour or hinder their desires. Human objectification, the denial of others, is the ground in which the various forms of violence develop: physical, economic, racial, religious, sexual, moral, psychological, etc., poisoning human relations and life itself.

A state of peace, balance and development is impossible without transforming the violence in the environment. It is necessary to break the destructive spiral of revenge and to make it possible to understand the roots of these conflicts, and thus to open ways for their effective resolution. Nonviolent communication will always invite transformation of the violent framework from which events arise.

In order to achieve its purpose and to be coherent with itself, nonviolent communication necessarily implies an incitement to simultaneous social and personal transformation. It is therefore in immediate conflict with the given social context. Here is the essential paradox: in order to resolve the root of a conflict, one must enter into conflict with that which motivated it. Furthermore, it will be necessary to adopt a critical view of everything that impedes the processes of nonviolence.

We are talking about a *deontology*,[5] a communication ethic, a direction of journalistic action that proposes overcoming all forms of violence through personal and joint action.

In this framework, any violent event requires the unmasking of its nefarious evolution, as well as any reaffirmation of its tendencies.

The latter refers, for example, to situations in which, in the face of a horrific or criminal act, increased punishment, the death penalty, the construction of more prisons, more police, social militarisation or citizen informants are encouraged.

Conflict, from the perspective and practice of nonviolence, no longer exacerbates hatred and guilt but highlights the structural condition of violent acts.

In short, violence, far from being hidden or misrepresented, is denounced and critically tackled in terms of a communicational ethic of

---

[5] According to the Encyclopaedia Britannica, in philosophy, deontological ethics are ethical theories that place special emphasis on the relationship between duty and the morality of human actions.

nonviolence. This ethic proclaims the need for nonviolent personal and social change. By its very essence, it comes into conflict with the establishment, with the passive acceptance of violence and revenge either as something natural or as situations that are impossible to change.

Best practice

Headline:	Violence against women increases due to the use of guns in the home
Media:	SomosMass99
Author:	Anayeli García Martínez for Cimacnoticias
Date:	December 17, 2020
Format:	News report
URL:	https://bit.ly/3KjPBcs

This news report connects two trends within Mexico: the overall increase in the use of guns and their use against women.

"The increase in the number of guns in Mexico has led to an increase in their use in violence against women, with 55 per cent of female deaths in 2019 having a presumption of homicide committed with firearms, revealed the study 'Femicide violence in Mexico. Approximations and trends.'

"Presented yesterday by UN Women, the National Institute of Women and the National Commission to Prevent and Eradicate Violence against Women (Conavim) the study noted a 13.4 percent annual increase between 2014 and 2019 in the use of firearms in households, and on public roads the annual growth rate was 18.2 percent."

By pointing to statistical data from a recent report, the article not only gains in informational quality, but also indicates a general overview that reveals the structural basis of the problem. In addition to the analysis, the article proposes ways out through two qualified spokespersons:

"'The increase in the use of firearms to murder women both in the home and on public roads demonstrates the need to strengthen policies against crime and the proliferation of weapons with a gender perspective,' said the representative of UN Women Mexico.

"Regarding this data, the feminist anthropologist and promoter of the General Law on Women's Access to a Life Free of Violence, Marcela Lagarde y de los Ríos, said that this study shows 'how (women within the feminist movement) are getting closer, building key pieces, articulating structures, dismantling processes in social life, all inspired by a political theory of gender to analyse these murders that for us and the whole world are called femicide, because they are hate crimes against women'."

Headline:	Being in the right place. A personal reflection after the murder of Willy Monteiro Duarte
Media:	Pressenza
Author:	Edoardo Calizza
Date:	October 1, 2020
Format:	Opinion piece
URL:	https://bit.ly/3xRyzzV

The article notes the painful circumstances of the murder of 21-year-old Willy Monteiro Duarte, who *"was kicked and beaten to death by four other boys physically much stronger than him between the ages of 21 and 26, in Colleferro, a town of 21,000 inhabitants on the outskirts of Rome. Willy Monteiro Duarte had intervened to defend a friend of his from being beaten."*

The author criticises clichés used by certain types of simplistic journalism, and then challenges the reader in an attempt to broaden the view of the facts, as well as expressing his frank and resolute opposition to the naturalisation and promotion of the violent act:

> *"I have read several articles and publications that, feeling sorry for the boy who was killed, wrote that he was 'in the wrong place at the wrong time'. This statement shocked me and made me reflect. I find it misleading and dangerous. Misleading, because it suggests that the problem is that he was there, not what was happening where he was. This is dangerous, because it seems to be telling readers that in such situations the best thing to do is to run away.*

> *"Where do we choose to be, what 'place' do we choose to occupy in the face of violence? Where is the right place, where is the wrong place to be in the face of violence when it manifests itself both randomly and structurally?*

> *"In a society that exalts violence, that puts it in the spotlight until it is assimilated into our consciousness as normal, inevitable, or otherwise acceptable, it becomes difficult to see who was really in the wrong place."*

Further on, the article establishes a proactive tone from a transformative ethic against the paradigms of violence:

> *"A violent model that finds its place, finds space and, even more worrying, finds recognition. A model which, on the other hand, needs room to be eradicated, day by day, neighbourhood by neighbourhood, school by school, to make room for a culture of nonviolence that exalts qualities diametrically opposed to those that are exalted today in people, in individual and social relationships. A culture that would educate from an early age to know how to discern, emotionally and intellectually, between what is in the right place and what is in the wrong place according to an*

internal and moral reference system that has at its centre the value of the Other, their freedom and their dignity.

"The place occupied by Willy Monteiro Duarte is the place occupied by thousands of activists, as well as other citizens, every day in every corner of the planet.... The place occupied by those who have a humanising look of the Other, of the marginalised, of all those who do not find space in the self-centred and self-celebrating narrative that dominates today's world. The place occupied by those who address the Other with kindness and consideration in a world that instead wants us to be opposition, untrusting and distant.

"The place that humanists occupy every day, aspiring to build a nonviolent reality, where the Human Being is truly the central value, recognising the right to oppose any form of violence that affects us, both near and far from this planet, with appropriate resistance."

Reconciliation as news

Journalism and communication have great power to establish and perpetuate meanings and ways of looking at reality. It is there, in the dynamics of the construction of meaning, where those who communicate play a preponderant role, given their essential link with information and their interpretative frameworks. In this way, they contribute to legitimising or delegitimising actions, structures and cultural practices in any society.

From our approach and on the basis of this cultural force, it is fundamental to integrate reconciliation processes in any of their multiple expressions, from individual stories to political processes, into the agenda of communication and journalism.

At the same time, this principle reinforces the need for an emphatic critique of all forms of revenge, whether overt or subtle, as well as a continuous effort to understand the mechanisms of violence in human societies, in order to facilitate their elimination.

For nonviolent journalism, the priority in the face of conflict is to contribute to its understanding and to show options that lead to its resolution. Thus, it is essential to analyse the motivations of the parties involved in depth and from different perspectives in the search for nonviolent options and alternatives.

There are forces opposed to positive conflict resolution and reconciliation.

These can arise from offences between different groups that are anchored in the past. That offence, mistreatment, injustice and misunderstanding, despite their remoteness in time, persist and the damage extends to the present: hence resentment, a state that prevents individuals or groups from acting with true freedom.

Resentment motivates revenge and debases one's own life and the lives of others. Through revenge, often disguised as a demand for justice, individuals and peoples believe that the suffering of others will serve to assuage their own suffering.

Resentment also tends to act from the logic of making an example of someone through punishment so that, supposedly, the destructive act is not repeated. However, this way of acting out of resentment does not at any point break the spiral of violence, but rather it feeds it again.

Entire societies and peoples clash again and again over images carried over from their near or distant history, which limit their ability to overcome certain conflicts. Thus, suffering and anger are multiplied by the fact that many of these conflicts are still ongoing.

Both the wounds that a society retains in its memory and the prolongation of the violence inflicted up to the present day must be healed. For this, a first phase of reparation is always necessary to promote reconciliation:

"This is not about trying to falsify the memory. This is about trying to comprehend what happened in order to enter into the superior step of reconciliation. Nothing good is achieved, neither personally nor socially, by forgetting or forgiving. [...] To forgive means that one of the parties puts themselves in a superior moral position and that the other party humbles themselves before the one who forgives. And while it is clear that to forgive is a more advanced step than that of vengeance, it is not as advanced as reconciliation." (Silo, 2014)

From the perspective of nonviolent communication, in each conflict it is necessary to detect the keys that allow the overcoming of resentment and the desire for revenge, which encourage the path of reconciliation. The story that is constructed has to present the need for reparation, inform about alternatives to achieve it, and suggest perspectives that project a future free from oppression and pain.

Best practice

Headline:	Christina Koulouri: Reconciliation between peoples cannot be achieved either by silence or by distortions
Media:	Pressenza
Author:	Marianella Kloka
Date:	November 14, 2018
Format:	Feature story
URL:	https://bit.ly/37Nv7fc

The article refers to the presentation of an educational material, prepared by Christina Koulouri, Professor of Modern and Contemporary

History at Panteion University, *"that aims to help the teaching of history in all Balkan countries, efforts that began when the wars in Yugoslavia had ended, a time when memories of war were very fresh, and the result was completed and published in 2016."*

The academic points to the influence of war narratives on the historical memory of societies:

> *"The experience of war in all versions leaves deep scars in societies, which are transferred from generation to generation. The memory of war is the organizing principle around which many collective identities are formed."*

From the outset, the author stresses the importance of dialogue and the search for common ground:

> *"About a hundred historians from different educational levels from 'hostile' or rival countries sat around the same table, talked and came to a conclusion around the narrative of the common past. The result of their work has been translated into 9 languages, including Greek, and is freely available online.*

> *"[...]Is it possible to transcend the ethnocentric narrative? How can we teach contentious and conflictual events to societies that have just experienced bloody war, genocide, massacres and displacement?*

> *"[...] Wars are interpreted in teaching as part of an ethnocentric narrative. [...] The traumatic experiences of wars stigmatize the present and create divided memories. [...] Thus, in the public sphere, 'memory wars' are being waged and there is a political abuse of the past and history by governments and parties."*

The professor alludes to the crucial role of education and continues with questions about the dilemmas in dealing with any armed conflict and its terrible aftermath. Finally, she offers some clues on how to move towards a reconciliatory approach to conflict:

"Will we advance in reconciliation, and then will the history of teaching be reorganized? Or will we use the teaching of history to arrive at reconciliation?

"[…] Should the perpetrators be forgiven in order to achieve reconciliation, or is justice more important? Should new generations learn about their past and reconcile with what their parents, grandmothers and grandfathers did? Do we need to remember or forget the traumatic events in teaching history?

"We must incorporate the above-mentioned aspects into the hegemonic narrative of history, i.e. change the narrative about conflicts. It is a necessary strategy in historical thinking in order to overcome ethnocentrism and recognize diversity. With regard to memory, the choice is not between remembering and forgetting, because forgetting is not something we can choose. The choice lies in the different ways of remembering. Reconciliation cannot be achieved either by silence or by distortions. Memory is alive, even under the veil of silence, especially when there has been a recent violent past. Education in history must undertake the difficult task of teaching about wars and conflicts to teach new generations how to deal with their dark past. 'The teaching of history can be effective and convincing only when it incorporates traumatic experiences and responds to the experiences of conflict'."

Headline:	The day Barcelona said no to violence
Media:	Pressenza
Author:	Raquel Paricio
Date:	August 16, 2018
Format:	Opinion piece
URL:	https://bit.ly/37NQaOH

This article highlights some of the most positive and hopeful aspects of the population's response to a painful event:

"This August 17, the city commemorates the first anniversary of the terrorist act that shook it, but it seems that the dominant media and political sectors have overlooked that what happened that day, in addition to being a terrorist act, was a direct assault on the deepest feelings of every human being. It was an assault that calls for nonviolence and no to resentment, to defend the right to intercultural and religious coexistence, to position oneself against the fear imposed by power.

"[…] 10 days after the terrorist act, Barcelona staged a massive demonstration of grief under the slogan 'No tenim por' (We are not afraid) […] The event was characterised by a diversity of voices with each one of them expressing their political position, but above all, the voice that won was that of not criminalising Islam, but rather the policies of war that, when put at the service of the globalisation of fear, lead to societies where military defence budgets exceed that of the defence of human rights.

"It was a citizen's call to clarify that we were not going to criticise a religion, culture or country, but rather the policies of war that at the time included the figure of King Philip VI of Spain accused of selling arms to Saudi Arabia."

The focus is on how people search deep within themselves for a reconciliatory sensibility in the most difficult of times, when it is easy to be driven by compulsion, fear, and the search for culprits and the desire for revenge:

"In this exaltation of love, people embraced one another, gestures of acceptance and brotherhood between cultures were palpable and declarations of pacifism were expressed in each section of the Muslim community. Such mass events, with peaceful slogans demonstrated by clear acts of affection, are becoming more frequent in Catalan society. Because since May 15, 2011,[6] the spark has been alive and much of society no longer wants to be a puppet of the fear that those in power are trying to instil.

"[...] Two months ago Barcelona organised a world meeting of 'Cities without fear,' a meeting of municipalities under a common banner, and here, in the demonstration, citizens had the opportunity to defend the slogan of that meeting: 'We are not afraid'."

---

[6] This is a reference to the social unrest against austerity policies imposed by the Spanish government in the aftermath of the financial collapse that destroyed the economies of Greece and other EU countries and which started on May 15th, 2011 in Madrid. The 15M movement that resulted was also known as the *Indignados* and led to the formation of the *Podemos* anti-austerity political party which rapidly achieved notable electoral success.

TOOLS FOR A NONVIOLENT APPROACH TO JOURNALISM

This chapter looks at different aspects of practising journalism from a nonviolent perspective. It is not a definitive catalogue, but hopefully serves as inspiration for creativity and analysis. They are resources for recreating a new style of communication that contributes to the construction of a different and better world. It is essential to point out the most important characteristic of communication for nonviolence: it not only transforms the surrounding reality, but it also profoundly changes the communicator.

Likewise, any conscious effort at internal transformation on the part of the communicator transforms the way they approach their profession. Overcoming internal and external violence contributes to the evolution of human beings and societies, which operate in permanent interrelation and mutual influence.

In committing themselves to communication that contributes to peace and overcomes all forms of violence, communicators must seek consistency between their personal conduct and the social message they send out, in other words, they must try to bring into alignment what they think, feel and do.

Thus, to undertake the task of working on oneself and together with others in order to achieve such unity is to understand that nonviolent communication not only aims at the transformation of the environment, but also involves the intentional transformation of the communicator.

This transformation is in order to improve the relationship we have with ourselves, our environment, our loved ones, society and with life itself.

In order to go deeper into our approach, we have to work on prejudices that operate as resistances or impediments. Thus, it becomes possible to understand how nonviolent communication begins with communication with oneself, with one's own inner self.

Our inner world does not stand still. What we hear, see and touch is tinged with what lives inside us. This interiority is what makes us different and creates the myriad of perspectives that exist in humanity, even if we share many cultural or generational visions.

With regard to nonviolence, one can quickly develop certain prejudices that hinder progress. Even if we think our look is free from them, we always start from previous positions and naturalised beliefs that seem immovable to us, which hinder the transition to other positions and other values.

The present day weighs on us and with it past beliefs and judgements about what we call reality. These ideas condition us all. Likewise, many common and naturalised assertions of the present time did not exist in previous times and will undoubtedly change in the future.

There are beliefs that take the form of automated prejudices and they drive our consciousness in a specific direction. For example, we could talk about the narrative installed by the mainstream media after the fall of the Twin Towers that *"every Muslim is part terrorist"*; a strong Western prejudice against the Muslim world.

Prejudices against nonviolence as a perspective from which to communicate

Below, we will review the lack of substance behind some of the main prejudices against nonviolence.

"Violence is part of human nature"

If this were the case, there would be no kind or compassionate people who cooperate with each other and help each other out, because our supposedly violent "nature" would prevent such attitudes. Since reality shows that humans can exist in thousands of different ways, human nature thus lies precisely in the possibility of choosing different attitudes, of choosing to resist violence or not, and thus also of choosing reconciliation and kindness.

"At the end of the day, nothing will change"

This prejudice, besides being discouraging and promoting a defeatist and impotent spirit, presupposes that society is immovable and that human beings have a perfectly defined, complete or definitive nature. This is increasingly doubtful, since it can be observed that transformation, growth and development are a permanent tendency in human beings, which has led the world and every individual in it to be shaped by history. What seemed impossible yesterday has been transformed by an invention, a new formula or another kind of knowledge. Everything changes at an astonishing pace. So the only thing that is permanent is change.

"What anyone can do alone is so minimal as to be of no use"

This prejudice shows how social systems seek to dwarf human beings who, as has already been said, are the makers of history. The actions that people undertake, individually or collectively, modify reality in one way or another. If these actions are humanising and are directed towards nonviolence, they are full of meaning. Furthermore, this prejudice prevents us from seeing people's most interesting virtues and how, from them, entire cultures and societies are transformed.

"Violence sells"

This prejudice is based on a commercial conception of journalism, as if the task of communication were to sell! The space of communication is not the marketplace, but the narratives, even if they have been degraded and distorted.

The predominance of violent information is linked to the need of the established powers to keep societies immobilised through fear. Moreover, by repeating and exacerbating this mechanism, humanity is increasingly anaesthetised and no longer feels horror at the suffering of others.

It is therefore essential to dissociate the work of communication and journalism from commercial rhetoric, promoting narratives of creativity, solidarity, and individual and collective transformation.

"To report in a nonviolent way is to distort reality"

This prejudice hides many others, for example, the one that claims that there is a reality independent of the eyes of the observer and, therefore, in the field of journalism, it is possible to report without interpreting. However, the most truthful information is that which shares with the public the point of view from which it is reported. So, if one chooses to be part of a current of nonviolent communication, this choice is made explicit, and people know how to frame the content that is delivered. On the other hand, the denial of the point of view in communication – supposed objectivity – represents serious manipulation.

"Nonviolence is passive and therefore counter-revolutionary"

Nonviolence as a moral attitude implies the permanent denunciation of violence, non-collaboration with it and committed action in one's own life, that of others and that of the environment in which one lives. There is no passivity in nonviolent activism.

Social struggles that confront the violence of the system with nonviolent methods are very numerous.

This is the case of the women who use their own bodies as a barrier against the advancing police, or the Indigenous peoples who march in silence to demand their rights, or the environmentalists who demonstrate every Friday in public squares, to mention just a few examples. Today, many forms of struggle for life are based on creative and nonviolent actions. Violence, on the other hand, plays into the hands of the system and feeds repression.

"Nonviolence is naïve and ineffective"

When has violence ever been effective? The enormous transformations that our world is undergoing are due precisely to the denunciation of injustice and violence and to people's discontent with discriminatory and violent practices by those who govern and wield economic power.

The new social movements and reference figures in the struggles for life, equality and freedom are seeking nonviolent forms of action. There is no naivety here, but rather a search to break out of the dynamics of power and repression, generating forms that break with the logic of repression and oppression.

A critical spirit does not prevent hope, the recognition of progress, of symbolic transformations, which open spaces for future de facto transformations.

Berta Cáceres, Marielle Franco and Vandana Shiva are a few examples among hundreds.

Constructing Information

Subject selection

This is a decisive aspect. First of all, this type of journalism emphasises all efforts in favour of peace, human rights, environmental protection, non-discrimination, nonviolence in all its expressions, and understanding between individuals and peoples. However, nonviolent journalism can tackle any subject as there is always something noteworthy to find in accordance with its look.

It is of great interest for nonviolent journalism to break out of the agenda dictated by the prevailing economic system, to echo the voices coming from the grassroots, from all those people and communities made invisible or violated by power, from those who step outside the official discourse and value freedom of thought and belief.

The news agenda must be opened up to issues that mobilise positive change or show exemplary attitudes of nonviolence in societies and individuals – new initiatives that, although initially small, are seeds of hope to the detriment of a monolithically violent narrative.

Simultaneously, the multiple situations of existing violence need to be critically addressed, aiming to reveal what are often their structural rather than particular causes.

It is essential to broaden our look and point of view in order to perceive, understand and show emerging phenomena that respond to new sensibilities and that clash with the prevailing narrative. It is necessary to go beyond the limits of our context, beyond our own training, beyond the usual news agenda or what we assume people are interested in.

As it is an approach, a way of looking at facts and reality, any event can be tackled from a nonviolent perspective.

To close this point, we would say that a nonviolent look is something that is learned and internalised through repeated practice. In this way, the consciousness becomes accustomed to looking for news or aspects of news that allow a nonviolent approach to be incorporated into it by the communicator.

Context

It is important to link the news items presented with content that complements them and helps to frame the events. It is essential to present a news item not as an isolated event, but rather to describe it in its development as part of a process. The term "process" does not refer to a simple linearity, but is understood as the geographical and historical structure of which the event is a part, with all its complexities and interrelationships.

Thus, it is necessary to contrast diverse and multiple pieces of information, which enrich the understanding of the events being reported.

Including a broad contextualisation facilitates the work of the information receiver. The human psychism is constantly working to integrate new content and stimuli into its flow, relating the data it receives to what is already in its memory. For this reason, framing the facts presented, both historically and geographically, improves the material and contributes to its reprocessing by the receiver.

This becomes indispensable at a time when there is an abundance of disconnected, biased, atomised, fleeting, manipulated and falsified content, which undermines the task of journalism and the social function of the press, driven as it is by economic, political and geopolitical interests, far removed from the intention of contributing to the common good.

It should not be forgotten that context is not neutral. Context carries with it content and validation. In the same way that issues and voices are chosen, certain contextual elements are chosen, quoted and highlighted in order to affirm what is being reported.

From our proposed approach, contextualisation must also be constructed from a nonviolent look, both at a critical and proactive level, in other words, emphasising elements that allow us to understand situations by prioritising human beings and enabling options for over-coming the factors that cause pain and suffering.

It is also key to relate the events in the flow of information in ways that open or reveal paths towards horizons that escape the logic of violence and hopelessness.

For example, in the face of frequent demands for justice in the face of violent circumstances, which often conceal a clamour for venge-ance against the perpetrators as a form of compensation for the harm caused, it is important to mention the progress made in recent decades in terms of transitional justice. This type of justice, present in ancient community practices of diverse cultures, places the em-phasis on the rebuilding of social harmony and offers ways for the reintegration of individuals identified as perpetrators of transgres-sion, without, of course, minimising the circumstances or the harm committed.

In terms of individual responsibility for atrocities, this type of justice highlights the structures of widespread and systemic violence prevail-ing in societies, allowing for more effective redress than simple indi-vidual punishment, offering alternatives to punishment that are sof-tened with possibilities for the future, and permanently demanding the modification of the patterns of individual and social violence that gave rise to those acts.

Voices

The plurality of sources and voices de-monopolises the interpretation of narratives and avoids the imposition of a single common meaning. In this way, the possibilities for analysis are broadened. Likewise, as already mentioned, the communicator's look is made explicit, which, far from implying a subjective deformation of what is communicated, clearly informs the receiver about the approach used, allowing them to draw their own conclusions.

Although we are talking here about plurality, it is necessary to counterbalance the existing imbalance between the protagonists who are usually consulted and other types of voices that do not find sufficient space in the media. In this way, nonviolent communication, by way of affirmative action, includes and prioritises looks that are commonly invisible, and includes voices and struggles that are normally silenced.

In addition, the options for diversifying voices need to be constantly reconsidered and broadened, moving beyond stereotypes in order to broaden diversity.

The choice of those to consult should be very careful, favouring the opinion of those committed to honest reflection, peace and constructive social change. In the selection of statements, priority should be given to those that not only give an account of what is most important from an informative point of view, but also those who propose solutions and alternatives linked to nonviolent activism.

The use of historical guiding figures serves a similar purpose, highlighting thinkers and leaders who have contributed to the elevation of humanist and nonviolent perspectives in different periods of history.

Nonviolent communication opens up spaces for the expression of different positions in the struggle to overcome exclusion and intransigence. The exception to this principle are those voices that promote hate speech, discrimination or violence. In this case, non-collaboration and non-broadcasting are forms of nonviolent struggle.

Language and meanings

As pointed out by the late Pressenza Journalist, Silvia Swinden in the opening to the chapter *Goodbye semantic violence, hello language of change*, in her book *From Monkey Sapiens to Homo Intentional*:

"Intentionality expresses itself in different forms. One of them is language. Through language we can glimpse the point of view of other people, their attributions of meaning and their intentions towards the future. Language is used to convince, persuade and threaten, altering in this way the point of view of others, but is also used to interchange and co-operate, developing collective points of view which are not the result of imposition but of joint activity. Language can be an instrument of violence or of development, and it is human intention that guides it in one or other directions." (Swinden, 2006, p. 116)

Language is not neutral. Each word harbours a world of meanings, intentions and configurations of reality. That is why we must always pay great attention to the words we use, especially in our role as communicators.

Semantic analysis, in other words the formation of meanings, from different angles, allows us to recognise and dismantle naturalised conceptions of humanity, the world and ourselves, thus facilitating the deconstruction of the prejudices already mentioned and many others. For example, to speak of race today is an anachronism, a flagrant discrimination, as it alludes to a conception of what is human based on the supremacy of one group over others, based on absurd justifications founded on aspects of body morphology.

Today, militarised language abounds in politics, in sport and even the way we talk about the COVID-19 pandemic, as if tackling such a challenge were a military operation, when strictly speaking all of the above corresponds to fields of human activity that are totally unrelated to armed confrontation.

We must recognise that militarised language has infiltrated us like water in a sponge, most of the time without us noticing. If we were able to sustain our discourse with nonviolent, inclusive and non-discriminatory words, we would be orienting our thinking in a new direction, thus also altering the course of reality by changing the way we perceive, name and structure it.

Showing the historical variability of language mobilises new points of view in communicators and receivers alike, which facilitates collective understanding. The same applies in the visual and audio fields, as in any other form of communication.

There are currently notable and positive changes in inclusive language, in which sexual and gender diversity stands out in a very notable way. Innovative ways of expression are being incorporated at a colloquial level and their official recognition is slow but unstoppable. This is especially so in languages which generally differentiate genders such as Spanish and German.

An example of the incorporation of these changes can be found in the German dictionary Duden, reported by Infosperber.ch in its article of 9 March 2021, headlined *"Masculine forms were never gender-neutral"* and written by Bárbara Martí:

> *"The Duden editorial team is revising the personal and professional terms in the online dictionary. The masculine form is explicitly joined by the feminine. A Mieter [male form of tenant] is no longer 'someone who has rented something', but a 'male person who has rented something'. And a Mieterin [female form of tenant] is a 'female person who has rented something'. For Ärztin [female form] it used to say 'female form of the word doctor'. The online dictionary now says: 'female person who, after medical studies and clinical training, has received state approval to treat the sick.' [...] This means that the generic masculine form of personal titles on duden.de, which refers to women, will disappear.*

"This has caused a storm of indignation, especially in Germany. Advocates of generic masculine forms spoke of 'gender gaga' and 'gender nonsense'. However, one can just as well speak of gender nonsense if the masculine form is to apply to all groups of people. [...]

"The basic problem is patriarchy, in which there is a more important and a less important gender. For example, if you want to increase the proportion of women in a profession, you have to start at different points. And one of them is language. It is always a component of social change and cannot be considered separately. [...]

"In Switzerland, public radio and television have been implementing inclusive language for some time. At first, it seemed laborious and forced, wrote Rico Bandle, who is known for his conservative views, in the Sonntagszeitung. 'But at some point you get used to it'." (Marti, 2021)

For English speakers who haven't attempted to learn foreign languages which differentiate by gender this can be difficult to grasp. By way of an example, the word *friend* in Spanish is *amigo* if your friend is male, or *amiga* if your friend is female. If you talk about, let's say, a group of 5 friends, all female, you would talk about your *amigas*, but if even one of the group of five is male, traditionally in Spanish you would use the word *amigos*; the male form takes precedence even though the male was in the minority. When someone addresses their friends in Spanish, it is increasingly common to see and hear expressions such as *amigas y amigos*. New gender neutral grammatical forms are also appearing, such as *amigues*, in which an 'e' sound replaces the male 'o' form and the female 'a' form. All of this generates just as much controversy in Spanish speaking circles as the trends in German outlined above.

In English, the generic word *friend* has no gender connotation whatsoever. However, traces of gender-specific language do remain in words that describe certain professions such as actor/actress, waiter/waitress and chairman/chairwoman. In the case of the former, there are those now using *actor* exclusively to talk about both men and women. In the second case, there are moves to using alternatives such as *server* which has no trace of gender. In the third case, both chairman and chairwoman are simplified by using the word *chair*.

Furthermore, gender neutral pronouns *they/them/their* (third person plural) have generally replaced gender specific pronouns *he/him/his* and *she/her/hers* (third person singular male and female) when one doesn't know the specific gender of the person being referred to. This is generally replacing the clunkier sounding pronoun *he or she*.

Conclusion, sign-off and closing

The information construction of a nonviolent story – the subject selection, context and voices, the language used, and so on – have the central objective of generating a register of humanisation in the audience, a link with others, a connection between the protagonists of the content and the people who receive it.

The final sentences of our productions should strive to be a powerful synthesis, highlighting the most significant elements and closing the arguments, summarising and articulating the themes that have been developed. Moreover, these final lines should open a door towards nonviolent conflict resolution and the overcoming of pain and suffering.

These are conclusions that – from what has been reported and described – point to horizons, to multiple possibilities that the descriptions and voices quoted underline. We ceaselessly mark out, indicate and explore the routes to reconciliation.

Headline

The headline of a story is fundamental, as it is the most viewed segment of all communication production. In an era of almost unlimited stimuli, the headline defines to a large extent whether the reader continues into the content or dismisses it, especially when it comes to digital sources and social networks.

According to the usual definition, a headline must be concise, easy to understand, but at the same time be expressive and forceful. But beyond its 'advertising' component and its composition, a headline is very relevant from the point of view of the editorial line. Many events and even the total content of a story may be valued or misrepresented depending on the way it is headlined.

From our point of view, a good headline emphasises humanisation, resistance and nonviolent actions, synthesising in a few words some key concepts. Otherwise, the headline should simply announce precisely the content to be developed. Under no circumstances should it be misleading, manipulative or inconsistent with the subsequent development of the story.

The comments made in the section on language are also applicable to headlines. Thus, the use of words or formulations that suggest warmongering, degradation, incitement to hatred or revenge is excluded. On the other hand, creative headlines that promote a sense of evolutionary, collective construction, or that make use of wit or descriptive poetry – without extreme abstraction – are welcome.

There is a maxim that may be useful here: a headline is a gift to the recipient, not a gift the author gives themselves.

Visual images

In the field of communication, images are not a random addition to articles. Images are central elements, whether as an opening, complement or extension of the contents of a written piece, or as a leading component in video productions and photojournalism. From the approach we propose, the intention of the communicator plays a decisive role in the treatment of images. The choice of image reflects what the author wants to show and, to a large extent, what they think and feel.

Any attempt to arouse morbid curiosity or to diminish the dignity of the protagonists is inconceivable from our point of view. On the contrary, we prioritise images that communicate dignity, beauty, diversity, joy and hope. However, we recognise that in denouncing violence and its root causes, it is necessary to resort to using images that show pain and injustice, without attacking or denigrating under any circumstances.

The production of images has a higher and more difficult purpose than showing a simple 'picture' of reality. It is a quest to unveil what is not in plain sight. In a sense, we are talking about generating the images of the future that we are pursuing, because without images of that future, its existence is not possible. A nonviolent image mobilises reality towards overcoming violence, pain and suffering.

> *"If images allow recognition and action, then according to the structure of the landscape and the needs of individuals and peoples (or according to what they consider their needs to be), they will, in the same way, tend to transform the world."* (Silo, 2003)

Communicational tone

People often communicate more with their body language, gestures and attitudes than with the words they use. Thus, what we write is sustained not only by the terms or language we use, but also by a communicational tone that conveys precise moods, climates[7] and mental atmospheres.

We have already said that the subjectivity of the communicator is always expressed, filtering into the choice of words and sentence structure. This subjectivity that permeates the whole structure of any journalistic production is what gives the communicational tone. Thus, in any given text, one can recognise the author who wrote it.

The journalism we promote establishes a careful relationship with readers, maintaining a cordial atmosphere and respectful language. It is a reflective communication, established with serenity, which seeks to highlight hope and reconciliatory elements, without denying the painful aspects of reality.

Each author must find their own communicational tone through practice, through trial and error, seeking the flexibility and dynamism of their own language in order to approach events with versatile resources, maintaining a certain level of disconnection with respect to their own texts. In short, it is a matter of recognising those subtle expressions of emotion that creep in between the words.

Often what is written can be enriched by quoting the voices of other people with different states of mind, which has the effect of balancing out what has been said.

---

[7] *"A diffuse emotional background or mood; any new object a person perceives when they are in a climatic state is tainted with the characteristics of this background or mood. A climate may be either temporary or situational, or it may be permanently fixed in the psychism. If it is permanent and fixed, it will perturb the whole structure by impeding the mobility of the consciousness towards more positive and favourable climates."* (Ammann, 1981, p. 122)

Humour and irony are also powerful resources for unmasking violence and calling for it to come to an end.

Collaborative construction

Another possible resource to incorporate, which responds to the spirit of the world we aspire to, is the collective construction of a piece of journalism. This tool of nonviolent journalism undoubtedly overcomes the competitive and individualistic zeal in which we have been trained. Collective construction powerfully broadens the look at any event and facilitates its understanding when viewed from different angles.

This exercise involves everyone giving the best of themselves for a common goal, resulting in a production that goes far beyond the sum of individual contributions. Community work in journalism is increasingly gaining ground, as it does in so many other fields of human activity.

Confirming the approach

How do we know if a nonviolent approach is present in a piece that was produced?

Below, we propose a table of criteria whose presence or absence can be identified relatively easily. In doing so, it is possible to verify how close or how far away any given piece is from our approach.

Systematic analysis of our approach

Category	Present	Relatively present	Absent
Subject selection			
Defence of peace, criticism of militarism, warmongering and belligerent discourse.			
Denouncing different forms of violence.			
Defence of human rights.			
Broadening agendas to positive signs.			
Context and meanings			
Denaturalisation of violence.			
Contextualisation of conflict/violence.			
Tendency towards resolution, reparation, reconciliation and overcoming the roots of conflict and violence.			
Mobilising, transformative approach, citizen protagonism.			
Language			
Use of nonviolent, non-degrading and non-disqualifying words.			
Voices			
Sources and testimonies that are diverse and not usually visible.			
Voices calling for nonviolent ways out, solutions and alternatives.			
Images			
Communicate empathy, compassion, dignity, solidarity. They do not denigrate or attack.			

Communicate joy, beauty, diversity.			
Reinforce nonviolent language and content.			
Communicational tone			
The atmosphere conveyed by the article is respectful, peaceful, reflective, hopeful and reconciliatory.			

NONVIOLENT JOURNALISM IN DIFFERENT FORMATS

News report

Short definition

A *news report* is arguably the most common format, probably the most basic format of news journalism genres. Different journalism guides and manuals offer more or less extensive definitions. However, they all agree on the following: a news report is an account of one or more current events, through which those events are made known to a group of people who might be interested in them.

López Vigil defines a news report as *"the report of a current event of collective interest"* and proposes three central elements that make up the news report format: a) the facts: the news story reports facts, concrete events, it is not a fantasy or futuristic story; b) current events: the facts that constitute the raw material of the news are facts of the present or, in any case, linked to it, which means that it loses relevance quickly, but it responds to the important need of communities to "know what is happening"; c) collective interest: if the fact is of interest to only one person, it is not news, it is a statement, an announcement, but not news. (López Vigil, 2005, p. 144)

The events reported in the news must connect with the interest of groups, communities and population sectors of an entire society.

A nonviolent approach to news reports

The content of any news report can be divided into certain generic blocks: key information, development and closing. The idea is to imagine the segments of each block as 'ingredients'. A suitable 'seasoning' is added to each one to give it the nonviolent approach, leaving the headline and the lead-in for the end. The following framework may be useful:

We will divide the construction process into parts: part 1 (key information), 2 (detail), 4 (context) and 5 (comments – optional) are the usual segments in a news item, grouped in the aforementioned blocks of key information, development and closing.

Parts 0 (subject selection and sources), 3 (selection of voices and quotations), 6 (review of discourse, language and tone), 7 (conclusion and perspective) and 8 (images and headline) are the ones where our approach can be introduced.

Below, we illustrate the parts mentioned above using the article *Colombians and Venezuelans unite at the border in an embrace for peace.*[8]

Part 0: Subject selection and sources

This is the first key place in which to introduce the nonviolent approach in preparing information. The aim is, as far as possible, to broaden the news agenda to include topics that are often intentionally excluded or made invisible in the media.

Efforts for peace and disarmament, scientific, social, political and cultural advances that benefit humanity, the defence of human rights, nonviolent resistance, the fight for decontamination and environmental protection, the denunciation of and the fight against any form of discrimination, the demands of peoples, initiatives and cultural expressions arising from the grassroots and religious diversity all constitute an interesting and broad initial spectrum of subjects.

In the article cited, clearly the subject is the mobilisation of Colombians and Venezuelans at the shared border in order to express their

---

[8] https://bit.ly/3Kt4NnO

desire for peace, at a time of high tensions between the governments of the two countries.

Similarly, the selection of sources is instrumental. It is necessary to pay special attention not to take as true anything coming from those who sow disinformation and confusion. There are also those who set out to manipulate information in favour of specific economic or political interests, so it is essential to unveil the intentions of your sources and the interests that motivate them. This is where it is possible to assess their reliability.

At a time when so-called "fake news" is multiplying exponentially, thanks to the rapid development of information and communication technologies, it is essential to verify sources, check data and sharpen one's look.

Part 1: Key information

This consists of the elements usually present in the first paragraph of an article: what, who, when, where, why.

Part 2: Detail

Paragraphs that expand on the information in the lead-in with more precise information about the facts, the protagonists, the circumstances and the development of events. In this amplifying paragraph, we can answer the questions: how and what for. This opens up the possibility for describing the events a little more and identifying the aims of the various actors in the events.

Example:

"Faced with constant threats from the Colombian and US governments of a possible military intervention in Venezuelan territory, several social, grassroots and political organisations have joined together in 'The Caravan against War.'

"The Caravan began its journey from the city of Bogotá on Thursday 14 February, with the destination being the city of Cúcuta on the border with Venezuela."

Part 3: Selection of voices and quotes

This is a special ingredient in our nonviolent approach. In the choice of voices we prioritise those which not only give an account of what is most important from an informational point of view, but also those which enhance the issue in a positive sense.

In our example:

"'We must insist that borders are territories of peace. That is why all the organisations that come together today are promoting this initiative whose main objective is to be against a war that is going to affect us all,' said Miguel Pinto Ardila, member of the Permanent Committee for the Defence of Human Rights."

Part 4: Context

As mentioned in previous chapters, the aim is to provide elements that allow a broader understanding of the events being reported, facilitating greater interaction with the information. Placing the central fact of the news story, characterised as current affairs, in a broader perspective and adding elements prior to or in relation to the central event, offers the audience the possibility of establishing relationships, connecting data, actors and processes, thus expanding the possibilities of understanding and developing their own opinion.

In our example:

> *"The Caravan against War is an initiative whose main objective is to raise the flags of peace on the Colombian-Venezuelan border, demanding a negotiated solution to social and political conflicts.*
>
> *"The first stop on the way to the border was made in Tunja, Boyacá, where local collectives supported the initiative with a petition for peace and actions for life.*
>
> *"After being received in San Gil by local farmers, the third stop for the caravan was Bucaramanga, where symbolic acts were carried out in order to bring the message of solidarity, union, integration and peace."*

Part 5: Comments

This part returns to the specific event and enriches it with further statements, opinions or additional information. It is not essential for all news items to have this part. The decision whether or not to add comments is at the discretion of the reporter who assesses whether or not this is important.

In our example:

> *"On Friday 15 February, the Caravan arrived in Cúcuta, where a vigil was held to demand that the governments use dialogue as the only way out of the conflict."*

Part 6: Revision of discourse, language and tone

This is the second of the three key areas when ensuring a nonviolent approach to news reporting. It is necessary to pay special attention to the language used, especially when external sources of information are also used. Eliminate language that could be degrading and filter out any kind of discrimination. Similarly, it is important that the story avoids any tone of resentment, moralising or pamphleteering.

Part 7: Conclusion and perspective

Highlight the informative ending and/or what is expected in the short to medium term. To conclude, a brief element is included highlighting how the event opens up any possibilities for change. The way in which each story closes is another key element of the nonviolent approach. In the conclusion, it is possible to highlight voices that favour conflict resolution, make proposals, open up possibilities and the future. It is also possible to emphasise the roots of the conflict and generate questions that lead to critical reflection.

In our example:

> *"Finally, on Saturday 16, on the Simón Bolívar Bridge, a 'huga-thon' took place to join together the resistance of both countries to war into one and to reject hatred and disinformation. A banner was erected declaring the border a territory of peace and solidarity between peoples, as well as a zone against war."*

Part 8: Images and headline

Of great importance is the choice of graphics, which should be coherent with the general idea, showing the place, actors, symbolising the best of the situation. Finally, with the headline it is possible to add editorial value in the direction of nonviolence or simply to announce precisely the information to be displayed.

In our example:

"Colombians and Venezuelans unite at the border in an embrace for Peace"

It is worth practising, as always, but especially in the inclusion of the humanising 'ingredients' that have been explained above and which by themselves do not necessarily appear in writing. On the contrary, this way of composing an article is a kind of nonviolent information architecture, which, once understood and applied, can be extremely useful.

Feature story

A format that is usually also classified as an informative format is the feature story. Undoubtedly, the fields identified for news reports are also useful for feature stories, a format that is usually more extensive because one of its characteristics is to go into the detail of events. A feature story reports on events in detail and, generally, with a time sequence very close to the events themselves.

Short definition

According to Costa Rican journalist, academic and diplomat Eduardo Ulibarri, *"A feature story is an in-depth piece of information; it reports on a current event, but it is much broader and investigates much more than a news report"*. (Ulibarri, 1994) For his part, Carlos Miguel Patterson says that *"a feature story is an informative work that requires arduous research into the subject to be published. It also goes into much greater depth than a news report with regard to the development and content of the event being covered."* (Patterson, 2003)

Thus, the main characteristic of a feature story is defined by the depth in which the event being reported is described. It is close to what we could consider a story, be it visual, auditory or text.

A nonviolent approach to feature stories

The sequence of constructing a feature story includes: the choice of the subject, the corresponding investigation, the elaboration of its structure, the production of the material, and its revision and publication.

One aspect that gives richness and accuracy to a feature story is to include interactions with the protagonists, so that – as with other formats – the choice of voices is decisive. This should include making contact prior to the actual production, obtaining authorisations for filming and photography, etc.

In line with the scheme used for news stories, and as with other news genres, the idea is to 'inject' nuance so that a feature story acquires a humanist perspective.

Subject selection

From the approach already explained on several occasions in this book, it will be easy to choose from the palette of topics covered, taking advantage of the possibility offered by this format to show situations in which different types of violence are suffered and which urgently require transformation. But also, the descriptive depth encourages us to look for cases that inspire and promote positive changes or that show exemplary attitudes in society and individuals.

In order to go beyond the simple denunciation of existing injustices, the aim is to contribute to a mobilising narrative and to allow the expression of the yearning for a participatory and nonviolent society. In the same vein, to give relevance to everything that contributes to overcoming the environmental, health, economic, political and social crises, highlighting any phenomenon that, however insignificant it may seem, were it to be published, could become a demonstration effect to be imitated and multiplied exponentially.

Preliminary investigation

In order to better understand the situation to be described, it is good to analyse it in broader contexts, either through a brief statistical analysis or by referring to related events.

The sources to consider should provide reliable material, so it is suggested to access data from internationally recognised public entities such as the many UN agencies, research centres, universities and non-governmental organisations with a long and recognised track record. If in doubt, check where your sources receive their funding from.

Consultation with government departments and sources close to activists on the relevant issues is also useful.

Voices

In feature stories about positive situations, the voices to be consulted are those of the protagonists themselves, without any mediation, which gives the feature story a testimonial force.

It is often interesting to ask about the original motivation, how the events or projects developed, the difficulties encountered and the achievements, as well as the prospects for future developments.

In relation to feature stories about negative situations, first-person accounts of the victims are undoubtedly fundamental here, and may include critical questioning of those responsible for the situation or those who could help to find a possible way out of it.

It may also be an important complement to include here a voice that helps to move away from the usual "victim-victimizer" duality.

Structure

The structure of a feature story comprises a brief informative introduction, with the main body being the narration of what the reporter wants to communicate, leading to a conclusion.

In the narrative we can point out elements of humanisation, such as the human capacity to overcome adverse circumstances, the dignity of those who fight for a better future for all, the collective factor, solidarity, creativity, and inspiration, among many other qualities to highlight.

Similarly, trying to highlight the intentions of those involved is essential in a narrative that aims to give a clear picture.

In the conclusion, as has been highlighted in other formats, the constant is that of opening the future, giving visibility to potentialities, possibilities, trends and evolutionary alternatives to the situation in question. Once again, this way of presenting places the feature story in a dynamic situation, which always allows for thinking in terms of virtuous transformations.

Production of material

In the production, it is important to take care of the protagonists. Thus, the request for permission from those who will be featured and the explicit invitation to make their situations public are very important in most feature stories.

However, there are exceptions to this rule in investigative reporting, where the exposure of a violent event allows for a degree of intrusion without prior permission. Even in this type of material, extreme caution must be taken, not only in protecting sources, but also not interfering in on-going legal processes. In such cases, a thorough investigation is essential, taking different sources, cross-checking and cross-referencing information with sufficient background documentation.

Something similar happens in situations involving a large number of people, such as accidents, catastrophes or situations of widespread violence, as well as in cases of mass demonstrations or celebrations, which makes prior consultation impossible. Even so, the principle of preserving dignity and personal integrity remains sacrosanct, and any morbidity or stigmatisation must be avoided.

It is recommended to record and photograph a lot, to allow for better quality editing afterwards.

Feature stories may require collective production across functions, which in turn stimulates the practice of teamwork, and which also requires internal qualification.

Edition, revision and publication

In editing, we will shape the narrative through the choice of the most suitable material. This aptitude is not only the pursuit of technical excellence, but also involves thoughtful consideration of where to place the emphasis.

To dwell on these matters would be excessive, as it is here that intuition and the creativity of each author come into play. As a suggestion, it might be useful to think of each feature story as a kind of short documentary or reality film.

As far as the final revision is concerned, the same applies as for other formats. What matters is the impression that this material will leave in the reader's memory and what kind of actions it mobilises.

Best practice

Headline:	Equatorial Guinea: Report of the accident in Nkuantoma (Bata)
Media:	Radio Macuto
Date:	May 6, 2021
URL:	https://bit.ly/3y0wW36

Headline:	The video *Tu vida con una renta básica* [your life with a basic income] invites you to imagine what society would be like if this measure were implemented
Media:	El Salto Diario
Date:	April 13, 2021
URL:	https://bit.ly/3vXGbOG

Headline:	Chile: against the regime and coronavirus
Media:	arcoiris.tv
Date:	April 14, 2020
URL:	https://bit.ly/3vSMMdh

Interview

Short definition

For Juan Cantavella, author of the *Handbook of the Journalistic Interview*, an interview is *"the conversation between the journalist* [or journalists, we would add] *and one or several people, with informative purposes (their knowledge, opinions or the revealing of their personality are important) and which is transmitted to the readers as a dialogue, in a direct or indirect style."* (Cantavella, 2015)

This definition hides four key elements common to all interviews, regardless of whether their purpose is more informative, interpretative or character profiling: the chosen subject matter, the voices, the dialogue and the information.

It is a dialogue, in other words, it presupposes a certain closeness, a basic atmosphere of privacy, although the participants know beforehand that it will be made public. Perhaps that is why Jorge Halperín defines an interview as the *"most public of private conversations"*. (Halperín, 2012, p. 14)

Asking, listening and observing are three central verbs of this format. Knowing how to do all three is the key to producing good interviews. Paying attention to the interviewee and treating them as we would like to be treated is fundamental, regardless of whether or not we agree with their arguments. But, in addition, this will allow us to ask new questions based on information that we were unaware of and which we consider interesting to go into in greater depth.

Regarding the role of the communicator, this can be very different due to personal characteristics or accumulated experience, but also due to choice. Regarding the attitudes of television interviewers, for example, Fernando Martínez Vallvey and Vanessa Irla Uriarte highlight the categories proposed by María Nieves García, according to whom, there are different positions: *"of equals, of superiority of the interviewer, of inferiority of the interviewer, and of intimacy."* (Martínez Vallvey & Irla Uriarte, 2017)

A nonviolent approach to interviews

From a nonviolent point of view, regarding the role of the interviewer, the attitude will always be "of equals," to which a friendly, neutral, but never aggressive style will have to be added, and always depending on the interviewee, the topics, and the circumstances that surround the interview.

In principle, it is necessary to choose the subject and the point of view of the information we want to give, which leads us to the voices.

The voices being interviewed are the focus of the format. The interviewee's expressions may be stated verbatim or summarised, but they are the direct source of the content.

We are interested in going directly to the source, as in other formats. We want to know the information first hand and, if necessary, give a voice to the voiceless.

With regard to the interviewees, there is an open debate today about whether or not the media are helping to "whitewash" and encourage certain positions by giving a voice to people and organisations that promote violence and discrimination, hatred and fascism, for example.

There is a fine line that is difficult to recognise between being faithful to information and helping to promote violence. This is what many leaders who are emerging around the world today rely on.

Secondly, the audience always finds information in an interview. Choosing one subject or another depends on current events, which will be determined by the agenda of the mainstream media or by issues that are happening but are invisible and that we in nonviolent journalism are interested in bringing to light.

First case: Positive news stories

It is the responsibility of the nonviolent journalist to give a voice to those who are developing projects that aim to build a different kind of society and who are not usually considered as much in the majority of the media.

At the moment, there are thousands of experiences that are hopeful examples that another world is possible. Today, hundreds of networks are being woven between small and large projects that nonviolent journalism is interested in making visible. Sometimes these experiences are very local, others affect thousands of people and are global in nature. It is important to interview the people involved, for them to tell us about their origins, the process and development, and what projection they have towards the future...

These are people and collectives who are already building the nonviolent future to which we aspire.

We have selected in this section of interviews the series *Women Building the Future, towards a nonviolent culture,* carried out by Pressenza's women journalists.

With a basic format common to them all, women from different parts of the world, working on a wide range of projects and taking the lead in writing history, were interviewed.

This series was also created with the aim of publicising the work of a few women, as a symbolic representation of the more than half of the population that continues to be discriminated against or silenced and who are shown as weak, without social projection, and only as victims or dependent on men.

In doing so, we are denouncing patriarchy and the whole system, as well as other particular forms of violence that differ from interview to interview. But the focus is on them telling us about their positive experience.

Basic Format
- The interviewee is welcomed, seeking to create a climate of closeness and trust.
- Introduction of the interviewee.

- The interviewee talks about the project/s in which they are involved.
- We go into a specific aspect that interests the interviewee in order to go deeper into it.
- The interview becomes more intimate, asking about the more personal reasons that led them to commit to this project.
- Finally, the interviewer is asked about the image of a nonviolent future to which they aspire.

Second case: Negative news stories

It is clear that despite our efforts to broaden agendas to events that can open up the future, lift spirits and grow, conflict and violence exist in many forms.

And as we have said elsewhere, we cannot and will not turn a blind eye to this. Such an omission would be unforgivable from the point of view of truthful reporting. Paradoxical though it may seem, violence, conflict and criticism are very important topics for journalism of the kind we are interested in.

It is the matrix of this violent and dehumanising system we live in that we want to transform. Therefore, it is necessary to talk about it, as well as its possible transformation.

A fundamental prior element to be maintained during the interview and in the final result we publish will be the tone with which we address our interviewee(s). We are referring to avoiding a pitiful tone, which is so common in certain situations of violence, in which the communicator identifies with the interviewee, thus encouraging victimisation in both the interviewee and the public, and encouraging a climate that closes off any possible way out of the problem that we want to make visible. Nonviolent journalism is far removed from tabloid journalism that does so much harm to the victims of certain situations and to the public who enter into a kind of complicity that is negative when it comes to conflict resolution.

The strategy we could use in this case is as follows:

We can ask questions, leading to explanatory answers about the root of the problem as well as the social and cultural contexts in which such conflict occurs. This can help to broaden understanding of the phenomenon and move away from positions that encourage polarisation, hatred, blame or revenge, for example.

Issues such as climate change, the mining of natural resources, colonialism, racism and violence against women, among many others, require us to ask ourselves about the future consequences of these trends.

In this sense, leading the interview towards possible solutions to the situation we are asking about can be of great help and would be promoting the approach we are interested in.

Asking the interviewee about the impact on their lives were the situation to be resolved can also be useful.

We are always interested in ending on a high note, something that opens the future.

We could use an example to illustrate the journalistic treatment of the situation. Let us take the topic of the mistreatment of and the discrimination suffered by migrants.

In an interview we can ask them to tell us about their situation and the violence and suffering they have experienced. We can then broaden the context: where they come from, why, and what do they want for the future.

For example: In your opinion, why do you think some people here reject you? Are you angry with them? Have you also found people who accept you, who treat you well? Why do you think they are respectful? Why do you think they are supportive?

And then we can turn the interview towards action and the future: are you in contact with other migrants who may be going through similar situations? Or with a group, organisation or association? What are they doing? What do they hope to achieve? How do you think we can overcome discrimination and violence?

Once we have the interview, we will define the central message or messages that we want to highlight and we will choose the headline on that basis, which will speak to the information obtained, the voices and the point of view that we have decided to communicate.

In a written interview, we can pull out certain phrases within the article that seem to us to be of most interest and that can highlight different sections or themes that have been touched upon, thus making the interview more dynamic.

Best practice

Headline:	Women building the future
Media:	Pressenza
Date:	2021
URL:	https://bit.ly/3s3CLZF

Headline:	Let's look with love, a project for the Wichí community – Part 1
Media:	Pressenza
Date:	September 19, 2020
URL:	https://bit.ly/3s2IgrE

Headline:	Transgender people trapped in the Ceuta immigrant detention centre: "We have escaped from one hell to arrive at another"
Media:	El Foro de Ceuta
Date:	August 16, 2020
URL:	https://bit.ly/37YrXVT

Opinion piece

Short definition

An opinion piece is a piece of writing characterised by the fact that it presents the author's personal point of view on a particular topic. Its most common aim is to draw the attention of the reader to something, inviting them to endorse this view and to reflect upon it.

It can usually be broken down into four sections:

- Headline: It should generate interest and curiosity in the reader. It does not always identify the subject to be dealt with, although it is advisable to include some allusion to it.
- Introduction: This serves to position the issue to be addressed.
- Body: Develop the analysis with arguments and examples.
- Conclusion: It establishes a position, invites reflection or suggests actions that move people.

The following resources are usually used in developing the text:

- Comparison: a relationship of similarity between two elements.
- Example: the introduction of a particular case that serves to illustrate the author's point of view.

- Authoritative quote: the words of someone who is a specialist in the subject are included in the text and serve to support the author's opinion.
- Generalisation: a particular situation is taken to a more general level.
- Questioning: used for a variety of purposes, e.g. to provoke, question an argument, raise options, etc.

This format of journalism undoubtedly emphasises the subjectivity of the writer, who nevertheless aspires to generate a more widely held view of a given subject. The personalised style, typical of this format, allows a nonviolent look and approach to be applied to any subject dealt with. Therein lies its specific value.

A nonviolent approach to opinion pieces

Part 0: Subject selection and opinion nucleus

In terms of subject selection, it is obvious that in addition to what has already been expressed in terms of the editorial priorities of nonviolent journalism, the intention and importance that the communicator assigns to the issue to be addressed is instrumental.

Likewise, although it is not an excluding factor, it is often a good idea for the subject matter to be opportune, either as a position on a currently newsworthy event or in the proximity of events that concern the public.

However, an opinion piece can also have the purpose of reflecting on issues that transcend the current situation, but which give a point of view on a general situation that could go unnoticed due to the pressure of the daily news.

Opinion nucleus: Once the subject has been chosen, the next step is to know what it is you want to say, or at least to have a rough idea of the general thrust of the article. As the article develops, new facets and even counterpoints to the basic idea may emerge, but it is essential to have a clear hypothesis at the outset.

If the piece is long, and includes lots of analysis, it is good to put together a skeleton of subheadings, which are like small chapters that contain the main ideas of what you want to convey. This is not necessary if the opinion can be condensed into a column of a few paragraphs.

In the case of long opinion pieces, it is not necessary to worry too much about the order of these segments at the beginning. The logical sequence emerges in the development itself. The same applies to the headline. If the inspiration for a headline was not there at the start, it can be defined at the end, together with a brief lead-in that summarises the content in a couple of sentences.

Part 1: Introduction

One or more paragraphs introduce the topic to be covered. This segment is key, as together with the headline and the lead-in, it is usually the defining element for catching the reader's attention.

Parts 2, 3 and 4: Plot development, considerations and contextualisation

In developing an opinion piece, some suggestions for dealing with the content from a nonviolent perspective are:

Arguments: In the analysis of the problem, leading your audience to see their co-responsibility and the possibility of collective and collaborative action in solidarity avoids blaming others and falling into paternalism or absolute external dependencies for its resolution.

Showing humanising elements in every situation, even in the most adverse ones, helps to lift the spirits in unhappy circumstances. For example, in the case of a critical article on the discrimination that still exists in some societies against migrants, also highlighting the supportive attitude of neighbours or activists helps to balance the look at the human condition.

Not everything is black and white, there are always interesting nuances and trends to highlight.

Likewise, humour, irony, creativity, joy and poetry are all elements that can lend literary style to an opinion piece in our nonviolent approach.

Contextualisation: trying to identify the interests in or behind the situation presented aids understanding and avoids both narrative naivety and feverish fanaticism.

On the other hand, placing the opinion piece in a broader time frame, as part of a process, strengthens the argument and contributes knowledge beyond the position taken. Seeing things in process facilitates the mobility of images, allowing us to understand that transformation is not just a possibility, but is characteristic of human life and history.

Likewise, when contextualised by relating the topic to associated issues, it enables other possible relationships to be looked at, broadening your audience's sensation of understanding.

Part 5: Revision of language and discourse

Language is not only a tool for speaking; words create meanings, convey emotions, they bring people together, or drive them apart, and they facilitate or hinder dialogue. For example, when referring to two political rivals, it is better to say 'adversaries' than 'enemies.'

In the same way, vocabulary automatically injects content, which must be noticed.

For example, saying 'government' is not the same as saying 'regime'. In the latter case, even without an adjective, some kind of authoritarian or anti-democratic behaviour is implicitly suggested.

From a perspective of nonviolent journalism, we are interested in denaturalising commonly accepted concepts or phrases that tend to paralyse action, such as 'violence is natural' or 'this is the way things are and they are not going to change', as we saw in the previous section.

Including positive words such as: dialogue, understanding, participation, collaboration, inclusion, community, communication or future, in the narrative, conveniently enhances the opinion piece, with the words themselves suggesting the paths to be taken.

Likewise, when criticising or denouncing unjust or violent situations, it is necessary to use concepts lightened of cruelty. Thus, as already pointed out in previous chapters, 'responsible' can replace 'guilty' or 'reparation' can replace 'punishment'.

The question is: what register do the words used leave in the reader? If it is a sense of violence, revenge or vengeance, they need to be reviewed in order to transform and improve the piece. It may be of great interest to have a glossary in order to replace commonly used terms that are far from contributing to overcoming violence.[9]

---

[9] There is an interesting glossary of terms and concepts compiled by UNICEF on nonviolence, peace and kindness that is worth reviewing. (UNICEF, 2018)

Part 6: Quotes, sources, voices, data, commentary

In an opinion piece, it is common to use quotes to illustrate or affirm positions. It is preferable to use phrases or concepts from thinkers and leaders who have contributed to the elevation of the human spirit throughout history.

While it is essential in an opinion piece to define a clear attitude, extreme polarisation moves away from the appropriate tone of the article, taking it closer to a declaration or pamphlet.

It is of great interest to incorporate or explore views which are usually silenced or given little visibility and which are fundamental to improving the sensibility of the article, such as those of younger generations, women and marginalised cultures.

On the other hand, complementing an opinion piece with data not only provides elements for better analysis, but also tends to strengthen the author's opinion. As in any other journalistic genre, a careful selection of statistical sources is essential, prioritising in general those coming from official or intergovernmental bodies that enjoy common acceptance.

Finally, if a bibliography or extracts from other articles are cited, clear references to the source material should be given.

Part 7: Position

Setting out the position you want to convey in a single paragraph gives you the opportunity to condense your opinion. This concluding paragraph could also serve as the lead-in or be used in social media to accompany the article in order to promote the opinion piece.

Part 8: Conclusion

In closing, which represents the final flourish, it is advisable to leave the point of view of an open future resonating. The future is not a consequence or an automatic repetition of the past, so an opinion piece allows us to try to show what the best future may be for the situation described or simply to open up apparently closed perspectives for the future. It is convenient to add an emotional touch in closing, a poetic reference, an open question, a key phrase, or to connect to the original hypothesis.

Best practice

Headline:	"The protests in Chile are a warning to any country that wants more neo-liberalism"
Media:	Pressenza
Date:	January 18, 2020
URL:	https://bit.ly/3kxt2XC

Headline:	Protest, repression and nonviolence in Greece
Media:	Pressenza
Date:	November 29, 2012
URL:	https://bit.ly/3y5OSt0

Headline:	Jordan, the tyranny of legality
Media:	Pressenza
Date:	September 20, 2020
URL:	https://bit.ly/3yeVYvg

Headline:	Good is what unites peoples, bad is what drives them apart
Media:	Pressenza
Date:	December 1, 2016
URL:	https://bit.ly/39oVMiJ

Photo story

Short definition

A photo story is classified as one of the genres of photojournalism and is essentially the narration of an event or the approach to a topic through a selection of photographs. Whether it is a news event or an in-depth look at a specific topic, the photographic narrative attempts to provide answers to the central questions of a news story: what, who, how, when, where and, as far as possible, why.

A photo story usually has the following elements: a) Headline b) Introductory text that summarises what will be shown c) The prepared photographic sequence d) Brief optional texts that accompany each or a group of images, by way of explanation or context. It can also be accompanied by a final sentence, which serves as a synthesis and conclusion.

Incidentally, the photographic material will be provided by the person who was present at the events and will have the corresponding rights. Their name must always appear in the credits.

Unlike illustrating an article with a few images, a photo story tells a story visually, from its beginning, passing through a pivotal point or central moment, to reach its denouement or end. So the photographer's look is fundamental, since it determines and gives coherence to the story. The light and shadows, the perspectives and the kind of focus will be key elements in composing the story.

A photo story is thus a record of an event or subject, narrated through a defined sequence of images that have been selected, so that the story, together with the look of the author(s), acquires an essential value.

A nonviolent approach to photo stories

As with words, images can also be shocking, repellent or sordid and can produce registers in the beholder that provoke feelings of rejection or even repulsion. This is why, when publishing pictures, journalism has a responsibility to try to predict the registers that will be evoked in those who see them.

What you decide to photograph reveals what you want to show. From a humanist approach, a good photo story is a visual narrative that unleashes emotions and sensations that mobilise the construction of a more human world.

A photo story of the kind we are interested in will highlight elements that bring out humour, colour, new and hopeful solutions, collaboration, solidarity, parity and inclusion. Photographs can show beauty, strength, complicity, resolution, joy, dignity, compassion and diversity.

This approach is about capturing those who participate in causes, audacious people who operate in the vanguard. It seeks courage in action. Photo stories always show the best of human beings, but also the pain, injustice, rebellion, oppression, resistance and the aspiration and need for a better world. A nonviolent approach always and above all respects human dignity, regardless of the context. We leave aside frivolity and superficiality to try to capture a shared gesture, a bright look and collective enthusiasm.

An important observation: nonviolent journalism does not seek to denigrate, ridicule or attack. Nor does it pursue violent actions, although it does not hide them. It does not emphasise the sensational, although it does try to make an impact. It rejects the morbid. It chooses its subjects with care, trying to communicate through visual language, revealing things that are not visible to the naked eye, for example, future aspirations.

Best practice

Headline:	March 8 in Quito
Media:	Pressenza
Author:	Walker Vizcarra
Date:	March 9, 2020
URL:	https://bit.ly/3vU8IVD

Headline:	December 17, Pensions in France: Faced with this historic mobilisation, can the government stand firm?
Media:	Pressenza
Author:	Pressenza France
Date:	December 26, 2019
URL:	https://bit.ly/3Lx5v4O

Headline:	Feminist collective *Las Tesis* among the most influential of the year
Media:	Pressenza
Author:	Laura Feldguer
Date:	September 23, 2020
URL:	https://bit.ly/3kxBO2Y

Headline:	Spain: "We put life at the centre to leave no one behind: Papers for all!"
Media:	Pressenza
Author:	Clara Gómez-Plácito Elósegui
Date:	July 21, 2020
URL:	https://bit.ly/3OQDkjy

TOOLS AND FORMATS

In order to facilitate the application of the approach in some of the most commonly used formats in journalism and using the tools described in the text, the following sections are proposed as guidelines and, in each case, a concrete training activity is suggested for their use. Hopefully, after regular use, all the elements will be incorporated into daily practice as a permanent methodology.

A nonviolent approach to news reports

Select a news report produced by you or take a news report from any media outlet. Following the descriptions used in below, check whether the selected news item covers the aspects described. Finally, assess and elaborate a news item, following the structure and description given. If you are doing the exercise in a group, share the results and comment.

Note: Sections with grey backgrounds are where a nonviolent approach can be applied.

Headline	A headline can include nonviolent editorial value or simply announce precisely the information to be reported. It can be defined at the start and amended later.
Lead-in	Summarises in one paragraph the main content or reproduces a significant paragraph of the story.
Selection of subject and sources	The aim is, as far as possible, to broaden the information agenda to include issues that are often excluded, have little space in the media or are intentionally made invisible. Among these subjects may be: efforts for peace, disarmament, scientific, social, political and cultural advances that benefit humanity, the defence of human rights, nonviolent direct actions, the fight for decontamination and environmental protection, the

	denunciation and fight against any of the different forms of discrimination. Likewise, demands of the people, initiatives and cultural expressions arising from the grassroots, but also ethics, philosophy and religiosity constitute a broad and interesting initial menu. Be careful to not pay attention to those who spread disinformation and confusion. There are also those who have the intention to manipulate information in favour of specific economic or political interests, so it is essential to uncover the intentions of your sources in order to ensure confidence.
Key information	This consists of the elements usually present in the first paragraph of the news text: what, who, when, where, why and how?
Detailed information	Expand in one or more subsequent paragraphs the details of the event.
Selection of voices	In the selection of "statements" or "quotes" we prioritise those that not only report the most important things in terms of information, but also those who enhance the issue in a positive way. In terms of context, the aim is to provide elements that allow for a broader understanding of the structure and process of the events being reported.
Statements/ quotes	Quotes and statements
Revision of discourse, language and tone	The tone, while denouncing violence, should not be resentful or "pamphleteering". Attention should be paid to the meanings induced by the language, especially if external sources of information are used. The discourse, while eminently informative, should suggest clear support for the story's evolutionary factors.

Commentary or additional criticism	After adding context, we return to the specific event and add further statements, opinions or information.
Conclusion	The conclusion talks about outcomes and/or what is expected in the short or medium term. As part of our approach, a brief element is included to highlight how the event opens up some possibility for improvement or positive change.
Images	Of great importance is the choice of images, which should be consistent with the general idea, showing the place and the actors and symbolising the best of the situation.

A nonviolent approach to feature stories

Select a subject of interest and write a feature story following the suggested structure and description in the table below. The story can be written down or recorded fou audio and/or video. If you can, discuss with someone else who is doing the same exercise and give feedback on each other's result, always bearing in mind what is described in the table.

Headline	It is advisable to include allusions to the subject, actors or specific geography. If inspiration for a headline doesn't come at the start, it can added at the end.
Lead-in	The lead-in summarises in one paragraph the main content or it alludes to significant expressions or conclusions. It is a complement to the headline and includes elements that usually attract the audience's interest in deciding whether or not to interact with the content.
Subject selection	The aim of a feature story is essentially to show situations in depth. From the point of view of nonviolent journalism, it is important to prioritise issues that tackle the need for change or to give

	visibility to alternatives and ongoing demonstration effects, as well as ongoing events that require more extensive reporting.
Interest/ Point of view	Define the purpose of the story and the point(s) of view to be used.
Research/ sources	Conduct research on context, actors and issues at stake. Cross-check two or more sources of reliable material. It is suggested to access data from internationally recognised public bodies such as the many UN agencies, research centres, universities or long-established and recognised non-governmental organisations. Consultations with government departments and activist sources on the relevant issues are also useful. If in doubt, check where your sources receive their funding from.
Voices	A feature story comes alive through the voices and pictures of the protagonists. In positive news stories, the voices to be consulted are those of the protagonists themselves, without any mediation whatsoever, which gives the story a testimonial quality. We show what caused the events, those who carried them out, their achievements and their perspectives. In negative stories, the first-person accounts of the victims are also essential and may include critical questioning of those responsible for the situation or those who could have been expected to help to find a way out of it.
Structure	The structure is made up of a brief informative introduction, the main body being the narration of what is to be told, leading to a conclusion. Develop the plot in a script. It is useful to create a structure with different subsections.
Production	Feature stories usually requires a collective production between different functions, which in turn stimulates

	teamwork, a task for which it is also necessary to qualify oneself. Collect plenty of film or photographic material.
Images	It is essential to treat people well. The request for permission from those who are to be portrayed and the explicit invitation to make their situation public is primarily a matter of policy. Exceptions to this are investigative reports, where the exposure of a violent event allows for a certain degree of intrusion without prior permission. Even so, extreme caution must be taken, not only in protecting sources, but also in interfering with on-going legal processes. Something similar happens in situations involving a large number of people, such as accidents, catastrophes or situations of generalised violence, which makes prior consultation impossible. Even so, the principle of the preservation of dignity and personal integrity remains sacrosanct, and any morbidity or stigmatisation must be avoided.
Conclusion	In closing, the constant must be the opening of the future, the visibilisation of future possibilities, trends or evolutionary alternatives. This way of presenting images places the report in a dynamic situation, which always allows us to think of virtuous transformations.
Edition, revision and publication	The narrative is developed through the choice of the most suitable material, not only in technical terms, but it also involves the editor's reflective look on where to place the emphasis. As a suggestion, it may be useful to think of each story as a kind of short documentary or reality film. As far as the final review is concerned, the same applies as for other formats. What matters is the impression and the register that this material will leave in the reader and what kind of actions it mobilises.

A nonviolent approach to interviews

Select an interview already published by a media outlet, be it TV, radio or print media, and analyse it according to the description in the template. Then, and only as an exercise, rewrite the interview you selected, applying a nonviolent approach, as if you were the journalist who prepared it. Compare the results. If you are doing the activity in a group, discuss with your colleagues.

Headline	The headline usually mentions the name of the interviewee together with a meaningful sentence, which can highlight the desired focus.
Lead-in	Describes the topic of the interview and a profile of the interviewee. This introduction allows for editorialisation from a nonviolent perspective.
Subject selection	Current news topics. Situations that refer to the need for change. Visibility of alternatives or ongoing demonstration effects. Events that require further analysis.
Research	Brief background research on the topic to be addressed.
Voices	Direct protagonists, who are invited to give visibility to their story or opinion. For analytical interviews, academics or observers the choice of whom, in itself, constitutes an editorial decision.
Introduction, presentation, welcome	Introduction, presentation of the interviewee, highlighting the relevance of their profile on the subject to be dealt with. Give a welcome.
Questions (positive news)	In the case of positive news, ask about the project in question, its protagonists, achievements, any specific aspect that is important to highlight, contexts, and the motivations that led them to commit to the project. And finally, ask about the image of the future to which they aspire.

Focus	The editorial element is introduced by highlighting the intentionality of those who build, the human capacity to overcome adverse circumstances, the collective factor, solidarity, creativity, inspiration, the hope they generate in the possibility of transformations, the humanising spirit of the action, etc.
Questions (negative news)	Ask about the situation of violence, those factors that generate pain and suffering, what response is being given, what should be done to overcome it.
Focus	Include questions about the root causes and context of the conflict, in order to broaden understanding of the phenomenon. Promote positions in the interview that express criticism of the violent matrix of the system and discourage hatred, blame or revenge. Avoid sensationalism and victimhood.
Questions (news story)	Ask about the events. Ask leading questions to extract informative details, the testimonies of people involved, the current situation and its possible consequences.
Focus	Be polite to the person being interviewed. Avoid complicated introductions and language. Do not ask leading questions.
Questions (analysis)	In the case of analytical interviews, delve into the surrounding context and processes. Clarify issues that are not obvious.
Focus	Get to the root of conflicts, highlight progress and obstacles.
Conclusion	In all cases, end with a question that points to the future with an empowering component.

A nonviolent approach to opinion pieces

Headline	It must generate attraction and curiosity in the reader. It is advisable to include a reference to the subject, actors or a specific location. If inspiration for a headline doesn't come at the start, it can added at the end.
Lead-in	Summarises the main content in a paragraph or reproduces a significant paragraph of the article. It should be written as the last step.
Subject selection	Within the framework of the priority themes of nonviolent journalism, the importance assigned by the communicator to the issue to be addressed is relevant. Although it is usually appropriate for the subject to be opportune, such as an opinion regarding a news event or related to events that concern the public, an opinion piece can also serve to reflect on issues that transcend the current situation.
Opinion nucleus	Once the subject has been chosen, the next step is to know what you want to say, or at least to have a rough idea of the central nucleus of the article. In the course of developing the article, new facets and even counterpoints to the basic idea may emerge, but it is essential to have a clear hypothesis to start with.
Introduction	One or more paragraphs introduce the subject to be tackled. This segment is key, as together with the headline and the lead-in, it is usually the defining element for the reader's interest.
Arguments	Develop the central argument in subsequent paragraphs. If the article is long, with a lot of analysis, a skeleton of subheadings is recommended. This is not necessary if the opinion can be condensed into a column of a few paragraphs.
Considerations	Showing humanising aspects in every situation, even in the most adverse ones, helps to lift the spirits in painful circumstances. Lead your audience to see their co-

	responsibility and the possibility of collective and collaborative action in solidarity. Humour, creativity, joy or poetry, are elements that are suitable for adding literary style. Not everything is black and white, there are always interesting nuances to highlight.
Historical/ geographical context	Giving historical context and framing a situation as part of a process strengthens the argument and provides knowledge. Seeing something in process makes it possible to understand that transformation is not just a possibility, but is characteristic of human life and history. Contextualising by relating the topic to other issues helps to establish possible relationships, broadening a sense of understanding.
Revision of language and discourse	Review the register of the words that are used. Words bring people together or drive them apart and they facilitate or hinder dialogue. Denaturalise commonly accepted concepts, deconstruct and reconstruct meanings in a nonviolent way. When criticising or denouncing unjust or violent situations, use concepts far removed from cruelty or revenge.
Commentary, data, quotes	In order to illustrate or affirm an opinion, preferably use quotes from thinkers or leaders who have contributed to the elevation of the human spirit in different moments of history. Complementing the opinion with data not only provides elements for a better analysis, but also tends to strengthen the proposal being made. Incorporating or inquiring into silenced views or those that have little visibility, such as those of younger generations, women and marginalised cultures, improves the sensibility of the article. When referencing books or extracts from other articles, the references to the source must be clearly stated.

Position	Setting out the position you want to convey in a single paragraph gives you the opportunity to condense your opinion and give it greater strength.
Conclusion	In closing, it is advisable to leave the point of view of an open future resonating. The opinion allows us to try to glimpse the best possibilities or simply to open perspectives to apparently closed situations. It is advisable to add an emotional touch (something poetic, curious, or definitive, etc.) or to connect it to the original hypothesis.
Images	The selection of images should be in keeping with the general idea, showing the place and the people involved, symbolising the best of the situation or pointing out what you want to transmit in a more abstract way.

A nonviolent approach to photo stories

Headline	The headline can add nonviolent editorial value or allude to specific issues, actors or places.
Lead-in	Summarise the content in one paragraph
Subject selection	Current news events. Denounce situations that require change. Give visibility to activism and ongoing demonstration effects.
Point of view and interest	Define the purpose of the photo story and the point(s) of view to be used.
Preliminary information gathering	Find out about the circumstances surrounding the event to be visually narrated.
Editing of the material and the story	Choose the most suitable material, not only in terms of quality, but also with a look at the contribution it makes to the story. Verify the lighting effects, which must be consistent with the different moments in which the situation was captured. Optimise image quality or impact by means of editing applications.

Post-production	
Introduction	Describe the story's subject or situation.
Photographic production	Highlight elements that bring humour, colour, new and hopeful solutions, collaboration, solidarity, parity and inclusion. The photographs can show beauty, strength, complicity, resolution, joy, dignity, compassion and diversity. Take pictures of those who participate in causes, audacious people who operate in the vanguard. Look for those who go beyond their limits, show the best in human beings and also the pain, injustice, rebellion, oppression, resistance, aspiration and the need for a better world. A humanist approach always and above all highlights human dignity, in any context. It leaves aside frivolity and superficiality, except in a critical sense, in order to capture the shared gesture, the bright look and collective enthusiasm.
Text	Short texts accompanying the narrative, either with descriptive or complementary features.
Review and publication	Evaluate, prior to publication, the register produced by the material, from an aesthetic, cognitive and emotional point of view. The story should respond affirmatively to the questions of informative accuracy, contexts, optical qualities, consistency with the desired story, and also leave a sensation which leads towards the construction of a more human world. It is interesting to ask others for possible improvements to the final product.

REFERENCES

Acosta Damas, M. (2017). Challenges of contemporary journalism: new narratives, media, sources and audiences in transition. *Alcance, 6*(12). Retrieved from https://bit.ly/3Ph9chs

Ameglio, P. (1998). Gandhi and the construction of civil disobedience. *Ixtus*. Retrieved from https://bit.ly/3LheiYg

Ammann, L. (1981). *Self Liberation.* York Beach, Maine, United States: Samuel Wiser.

Amnesty International. (2020). *Human rights in Africa: Review of 2019.* London: Amnesty International. Retrieved from Amnesty International: https://bit.ly/3FS4keh

Aristotle. (1931). *The Works of Aristotle Translated into English under the Editorship of W.D. Ross, M.A., Hon. LL.D. (Edin.), Volume 3.* Oxford, United Kingdom: Clarendon Press.

Bonnin, J. E. (2015). Los discursos sobre la reconciliación:. In C. Feld, & M. Franco, *Democracia, hora cero: Actores, políticas y debates en los inicios de la posdictadura* (pp. 225-268). Buenos Aires, Argentina: Fondo de Cultura Económica de Argentina, S.A.

Brito Lorenzo, Z. (2008). Educación popular, cultura e identidad desde la perspectiva de Paulo. *Paulo Freire. Contribuciones para la pedagogía*, pp. 29-45.

Byrne, A. (2006). Intentionality. In J. Sarkar, & J. Pfeifer (Eds.), *The Philosophy of Science: an encyclopedia.* Routledge. Retrieved from https://bit.ly/3shvJ3x

Cantavella, J. (2015). *Manual de la entrevista periodística [The Handbook of Journalistic Interviews].* Madrid, Spain: Editorial Ariel.

Carsen, C. (2001). *The Autobiography of Martin Luther King, Jr.* New York, United States: Grand Central Publishing.

Caston, V. (1998). Connecting Traditions: Augustine and the Greeks on Intentionality. (E. Sosa, Ed.) *Philosophy and Phenomenological Research, 58*(2), 249–298. Retrieved from https://bit.ly/3wmT1Yi

Caston, V. (2019). Intentionality in Ancient Philosophy. In E. Zalta (Ed.), *The Stanford Encyclopedia of Philosophy.* Metaphysics Research Lab, Stanford University. Retrieved from https://stanford.io/37rDYmx

Feres, A. (Director). (2019). *Ellas sienten que amanecerá* [Motion Picture].

Fischer, L. (1951). *The Life of Mahatma Gandhi.* London, United Kingdom: J. Cape.

Freire, P. (2005). *Pedagogy of the Oppressed.* (M. B. Ramos, Trans.) New York, United States: The Continuum International Publishing Group Inc. Retrieved from https://bit.ly/3wDia1x

Galtung, J. (1969). Violence, Peace and Peace Research. *Journal of Peace Research*, 167-191.

Galtung, J. (1990). Cultural Violence. *Journal of Peace Research*, 291-305.

Grandmothers of Plaza de Mayo. (2017). *Comunicado de Abuelas de Plaza de Mayo: Rechazamos la idea de "reconciliación" con los genocidas que impulsa la Conferencia Episcopal Argentina*. Retrieved from Movimiento Socialista de los Trabajadores: https://bit.ly/3tQZuby

Halperín, J. (2012). *La Entrevista Periodística [The Journalistic Interview].* Buenos Aires, Argentina: Aguilar.

Husserl, E. (1960). *Cartesian Meditations.* Dordrecht, Netherlands: Springer-Science+Business Media, B.V.

Husserl, E. (1983). *Ideas pertaining to a pure phenomenology and to a phenomenological philosophy.* Dordrecht, Netherlands: Kluwer Academic Publishers.

Jacob, P. (2019). Intentionality. In E. Zalta (Ed.), *The Stanford Encyclopedia of Philosophy.* Metaphysics Research Lab, Stanford University. Retrieved from https://stanford.io/3Pat45U

Jahnen, L. (Director). (2016). *Beyond Revenge* [Motion Picture].

León, J., Álvarez, R., & Karam, T. (2000). Comunicación popular y educación: el caso del equipo de comunicación educativa de Madrid. *Razón y Palabra*. Retrieved from https://bit.ly/37nbj1U

López Vigil, J. I. (2005). *Manual Urgente para radialistas apasionados [An urgent manual for passionate radio journalists]*. Quito, Ecuador.

Lynch, J., & Galtung, J. (2010). *Reporting Conflict: new directions in peace journalism.* St. Lucia, Australia: University of Queensland Press.

Lynch, J., & McGoldrick, A. (2014). *Peace Journalism.* London, UK: Hawthorn Press Limited.

Marquina, A. (2003). *Contributions for a nonviolent education – theory and practice of Universalist Humanism.* Santiago, Chile: Virtual Ediciones.

Marti, B. (2021, March 9). *Die männlichen Formen waren nie geschlechtsneutral.* Retrieved from Infosperber: https://bit.ly/37TBnBZ

Martin-Barbero, J. (2012). De la comunicación a la cultura: Perder el "objeto" para ganar el proceso. *Signo pensam*, pp. 76-84. Retrieved from https://bit.ly/3DaRk1Q

Martínez Pacheco, A. (2016). La violencia. Conceptualización y elementos para su estudio. *Política y cultura*(46), pp. 7-31. Retrieved from https://bit.ly/3pZ3sxA

Martínez Vallvey, F., & Irla Uriarte, V. (2017). El entrevistador en televisión: actitudes y estilos [The TV interviewer: attitudes and styles]. *Estudios sobre el Mensaje Periodístico, 23*(2), pp. 1247-1263.

May, R. (1974). *Love and Will.* New York, United States: Dell Publishing Co. Inc.

Mendez, L. (2015). *Violence and Nonviolence.* Buenos Aires, Argentina: Espacio Editorial.

Milgram, S. (1963). Behavioral Study of obedience. *The Journal of Abnormal and Social Psychology*, 371-378.

Milgram, S. (1973, December). The Perils of Obedience. *Harper's Magazine*, pp. 62-78.

Nietzsche, F. W. (1887). *The genealogy of morals.* New York, United States: Boni and Liveright.

Novotny, H. (2007). *Intentionality in human and universal evolution.* Retrieved from Meditations, Portal for Practical Philosophy: https://bit.ly/3wfAwDQ

Oberg, J. (2021). *Goodbye Peace. Worldmoires Into A Peaceful Future.* Lund, Sweden.

Ortega y Gasset, J. (1961). *The Modern Theme.* New York, United States: Harper and Row.

Patterson, C. M. (2003). El buen reportaje, su estructura y características [The good feature story, its structure and characteristics]. *Revista Latina de Comunicación Social, 56.* Retrieved from https://bit.ly/3MEwiw5

Rampoldi, M. (2015). *Entrevista sobre la superación de la cultura de la venganza.* Retrieved from Pressenza: https://bit.ly/3u0GeKd

Sharp, G. (2012). *Sharp's Dictionary of Power and Struggle.* Oxford: Oxford University Press.

Silo. (1996). *Letters to My Friends.* San Diego, United States: Latitude Press. Retrieved from https://bit.ly/3w9kwU5

Silo. (1999). *Humanize the Earth.* San Diego, United States: Latitude Press. Retrieved from https://bit.ly/3kQN1k1

Silo. (2000). Regarding what is human. In Silo, *Silo Speaks.* San Diego, United States: Latitude Press. Retrieved from https://bit.ly/3MWJKvA

Silo. (2003). *Contributions to Thought.* San Diego, United States: Latitude Press. Retrieved from https://bit.ly/3yn0mZu

Silo. (2014). Psicologia IV [Psychology IV]. In Silo, *Apuntes de Psicologia [Psychology Notes]*. Santiago, Chile: Virtual ediciones.

Silo. (2014). San Francisco Speech. *Coffee with Silo and the Quest for Meaning in Life*. Budapest, Hungary: Mikebuda Park of Study and Reflection.

Silo. (2014). *Silo in the Open Air.* Madrid, Spain: Editorial León Alado.

Silo. (2022). Violence. In Silo, *Complete Works Volume 2* (pp. 405-406). London, United Kingdom: RelayNET. Retrieved from https://bit.ly/3LPEiX3

Swinden, S. (2006). *The Genealogy of Nonviolence.* London, United Kingdom: Adonis & Abbey Publishers Limited.

Ulibarri, E. (1994). *Idea y Vida del Reportaje [Idea and Life of a Feature Story].* Mexico City, Mexico: Editorial Trillas.

UNESCO. (1980). *Many Voices, One World.* London, United Kingdom: Kogan Page. Retrieved from https://bit.ly/3JmjlWt

UNICEF. (2018). *Non-violence, peace and kindness: A glossary of terms.* Retrieved from UNICEF: https://bit.ly/3MFuuTN

United Nations. (1948). *Universal Declaration of Human Rights.* Retrieved from United Nations: https://bit.ly/3vUuyJK

Vázquez, M. (2018, August 30). *We don't do alternative journalism, we tell people's stories.* Retrieved from sangrre.com.ar: https://bit.ly/3ikVniK

World Health Organization. (2002). *World report on violence and health: summary.* Geneva, Switzerland: World Health Organization.

Youngblood, S. (2017, December 14). What is Peace Journalism? Retrieved from https://rb.gy/pldkm6

AUTHOR BIOGRAPHIES

Pía Figueroa Edwards, Chilean, has a degree in Art History and is an expert in ecology. She entered politics in the 1980s, participating in the founding of the Humanist Party. After the return to democracy, she became Undersecretary of State in the cabinet of President Patricio Aylwin, representing Chile in various international negotiations related to climate change, the Montreal Protocol and the Antarctic Treaty, as well as running twice for parliament. She was president of the Laura Rodriguez Foundation, dedicated to gender, educational, communication, environmental and health issues, and to the realisation of numerous social projects.

She worked as environmental advisor to the Minister of Agriculture, Director of Extension of the Educares University. Since 1994 she has directed the International Environmental Fair, *EcoFeria*. She is vice-president of the Pangea Foundation and director of *TempoConsultores*. She collaborates with various academic bodies and institutions, the media, private companies and non-governmental organisations. She advises national and foreign companies in the areas of communication, training, event organisation and the environment. From 2008 to date, she has been co-director of Pressenza, international press agency.

She writes regularly, is an executive producer of television documentaries and has produced several research monographs.

She has published three books, translated and edited in different languages, which form part of the current of thought known as Universalist Humanism.

Nelsy Lizarazo Castro, of Colombian and Ecuadorian nationality, has a postgraduate degree in Political Science and International Relations and an undergraduate degree in Philosophy and Literature. As a communicator and educator, she worked for twelve years, over two different periods, in ALER, the Latin American Association of Popular Education and Communication. She is a university lecturer and founder of Pressenza, as well as editor in the Ecuadorian bureau and, for the last five years, has been a co-producer of the radio programme *Cuatro Elementos [Four Elements]*, which focuses on the analysis of international events.

Juana Pérez Montero has a degree in journalism from the Faculty of Information Sciences at the Complutense University of Madrid. She has worked in the written press and radio. Committed to Siloism and nonviolence from a very young age, she edited the periodical *The Humanist* in Spain between 1984 and 1986. She has developed her journalistic work collaborating with different groups, social movements and spiritual expressions. Her commitment to collective creation has led her to participate in the production of documentaries, books and monographs, as well as in the construction of networks of activists who advocate for an unconditional universal basic income, nuclear disarmament, dialogue and reconciliation between individuals and peoples.

Her life and work is an incessant quest to learn and contribute to the opening of new personal and social paths. She has held different positions in Pressenza since its inception and today she is part of the team of editors and journalists. She combines these activities with poetry, research and writing on different subjects.

Tony Robinson has been an activist for peace and nonviolence since his student days at Cambridge University, where he met the Humanist Movement. In 2009, he joined World without Wars and Violence and took part in the first World March for Peace and Nonviolence which campaigned for the elimination of nuclear arsenals and all forms of violence.

Since his participation in the World March, Tony has been first a writer, then an editor and finally a co-director for Pressenza, International Press Agency, specialising in matters of peace and disarmament, closely following all the developments that led to the 2017 UN

Treaty on the Prohibition of Nuclear Weapons and its subsequent entry into force. In 2019, he produced the award-winning documentary film, *The Beginning of the End of Nuclear Weapons,* with director Álvaro Orús. Until 2022, he was the operations director for the Middle East Treaty Organization which campaigns to eliminate all weapons of mass destruction from the Middle East and on the Coordinating Committee of Abolition 2000, the Global Network to Eliminate Nuclear Weapons.

Javier Tolcachier is a researcher at the World Centre for Humanist Studies. He is a columnist and member of the founding team of Pressenza, International Press Agency. His works include the books *Memories of the Future, The Fall of the Dragon and the Eagle, Humanising History* and *Trends,* as well as papers, articles, studies and monographs that attempt to apply a humanist look to diverse fields of human activity. He has been involved in the Humanist Movement for four decades and lives in Córdoba, Argentina, his hometown.

9 798218 182892